High and
Holy Days

A Book of Jewish Wisdom

Rabbi Andrew Goldstein
and
Rabbi Charles Middleburgh

CANTERBURY
PRESS
Norwich

© Andrew Goldstein and Charles Middleburgh 2010

First published in 2010 by the Canterbury Press Norwich
Editorial office
13–17 Long Lane,
London, EC1A 9PN, UK

Canterbury Press is an imprint of Hymns Ancient and
Modern Ltd (a registered charity)
13A Hellesdon Park Road,
Norwich, NR6 5DR, UK

www.scm-canterburypress.co.uk

British Library Cataloguing in Publication data

A catalogue record for this book is available
from the British Library

978-1-85311-994-1

Printed and bound in Great Britain by
J. F. Print Ltd

We are grateful to Judith Littman and the office staff at Northwood & Pinner Liberal Synagogue for their support during this project; to Dr Piet van Boxel, Hebrew and Judaica Curator at the Bodleian Library, Oxford; and to our mentors, Rabbi John D. Rayner, z"l, and Professor Eric L. Friedland, for their inspiration, guidance and help on our liturgical odyssey. We also express our appreciation for the support and help we have received from Christine Smith, Publishing Director, and Rebecca Hills, Editorial and Rights Administrator, at SCM Canterbury Press. Above all, we acknowledge with the deepest gratitude the forbearance and support of our wives, Sharon and Gilly, over the many years that we have spent shut away in our studies for countless hours working on this and other similar projects.

The Editors

Contents

Introduction

Of the festivals in the Jewish year none are more significant than the two known to Jews as the High Holy Days, Rosh Hashanah (the New Year), and Yom Kippur (the Day of Atonement). Rosh Hashanah occurs on the first day of the month of Tishri, the seventh month in the Hebrew calendar, and Yom Kippur on the tenth of the month. The earliest biblical calendar commenced the year in the spring, and this is reflected by the fact that Jews still count the months of the year from that season. When the Israelites went into exile in Babylon in the sixth century BCE they adopted the Babylonian calendar whose New Year and most important festivals took place in the autumn.

On their return from exile, the Israelites brought with them the Babylonian names for the months of the year and the lunar calendar by which we still live our religious lives today, and to which the entire pattern of Judaism is pegged.

Ten days separate Rosh Hashanah and Yom Kippur, and they are known as Aseret Yemey Teshuvah, the Ten Days of Penitence. This is the most serious season of the year, when we review our behaviour in the previous twelve months, acknowledge our sins and failings, actively seek the forgiveness of those we have wronged and repent and pray to God for forgiveness. It is one of Judaism's most fundamental teachings that we pray to God directly, without any intermediary, and if our repentance is sincere and our resolve to lead a better life is genuine God *will* forgive us and we can start afresh with a clean slate.

Over the centuries, however, the view developed that ten days of self-examination might not be enough for the average person to set their lives in order, and as a result it was ordained that the period of reckoning would begin on the first day of the month preceding Rosh Hashanah, which is called Elul.

In Elul, according to Jewish tradition, special penitential prayers called Selichot may be recited in addition to the regular liturgy, building to a crescendo in a midnight service entirely of penitential prayers the Saturday night before Rosh Hashanah.

The Elul recitation of special selichot inspired us to choose the theme of 40 Days of Repentance (30 days of Elul plus 10 of penitence) for this anthology. We have selected a subject for each day, some general, some specific to the actual day, and chosen seven readings from all periods of Jewish history, ancient, medieval and modern linked to the subject. Some are prose, some poetry, some are prayers, some meditations, some spiritual or theological observations, and the passages are of varying length.

We hope that readers of the anthology will follow the pattern of reading the theme for each day, perhaps at the start of the day, so that its contents may be contemplated as the day unfolds or as an accompaniment to religious services during this period, though we know that others will choose a method that suits them and their purpose.

The idea for this anthology began when we worked on producing a High Holy Day prayer book (Machzor Ruach Chadashah, Liberal Judaism 2003) in the process of which we identified many more passages than we could feasibly include. While the origin of this book lay in the creation of a Jewish liturgy for a specific season, we hope that it will be seen as a valuable source of religious meditation and spiritual inspiration for Jew and non-Jew alike throughout the year.

Andrew Goldstein   Charles Middleburgh

Most of the biblical texts used in this anthology are based on the New Revised Standard Version, 1995 (NRSV) or the Jewish Publication Society Tanakh, 1999 (JPS) translations of the Hebrew Bible: some are in gender specific and others in non-gender specific English. In one or two cases, for subjective reasons of aesthetics, we have chosen to use the King James Bible.

For Gilly

נפשי קשורה בנפשה

And in loving memory of my father

Chaim

CHM

For Sharon

דודי לי ואני לה

AG

I

New Moon of Elul

Every new moon announces the beginning of a new Jewish month and is traditionally marked by a minor holiday called Rosh Chodesh. The month of Elul has a particular religious character as it leads up to Rosh Hashanah, the Jewish New Year. It is a month of spiritual preparation, beginning the process of *teshuvah*, repentance, of returning to God.

אֲנִי לְדוֹדִי וְדוֹדִי לִי

The wise prepare themselves with repentance (*teshuvah*) prayer and charity during the month of Elul. Then they will be ready to appear before God on Rosh Hashanah. The initial Hebrew letters of the verse אֲנִי לְדוֹדִי וְדוֹדִי לִי – "I am my beloved's and my beloved is mine," make up the word אֱלוּל, Elul. If we genuinely desire to return to God in *teshuvah*, then God's love will be stirred towards us and our *teshuvah* will be accepted.

Moses ben Abraham of Premsla

Prayer for the New Month – Rosh Hodesh Elul
Ha Rahaman, O One of loving warmth,
be with us as we walk with
and learn from Elul.

The month of Elul
awakes each dawn,
to the voice of shofar,
and rouses each midnight,
to the music of prayer.
The month of Elul
bears
scent of wild rose and
sound of the departing wings
of turtle doves.

The month of Elul
time of readying
time of shaping understanding
time of picking ripe figs.

Elul stands
holding
remnants of summer heat and
hot desert winds which
scatter shards of thistles, grasses, and vegetable seeds
wildly into the air.
Elul stands
holding
new born autumn fog and
freshly woven dew which
shoos scent of carob and tamarisk blooms
mischievously into evening breeze
driving insect life afrenzy.
Thus Elul instructs us
that the pieces that have died within us
bear seeds of future possibilities,
and that when parched,
rains of restoration follow.

NEW MOON OF ELUL

Elul bids us learn from the earth,
who moves gracefully into season of ripening
who readies for her winter.
Elul bids us follow in her wake
and take stock of our vintage,
and review our winter larders.
Our storage of woolens,
to check both inner and outer resources, and
to move one step
beyond.

Elul enjoins us to forgive.
For she, wisened with age,
knows that accounts unsettled act
like the small tear in a sack of flour
from which a steady stream of wheat pours
surreptitiously
until the sack lies depleted,
thus too do unforgiven deeds and words
drain and alter our form.

Elul calls us
to forgive, to forgive,
to forgive others whom we have wounded
wittingly and unwittingly
by words, and by actions.
She bids us speak words, which stick in our craw like
    leftover morning gruel clings to the pot, and
        to ask forgiveness, and
        to grant forgiveness.

Elul calls us
to forgive,
to forgive ourselves whom we have wounded
wittingly and unwittingly

by words, and by actions.
She bids us look at ourselves,
which stings like lemon juice in an open wound,
and to ask forgiveness, and
    to grant forgiveness.

Holy One
as the new month nears,
renew us.
Gift us with length of days,
a life of peace,
of goodness,
a life of blessing,
a life which can sustain us,
a life we can face with vigour,
a life where we touch awe,
a life where we struggle,
    aware of when we get off track,
a life without shame,
a life of richness,
of honour,
a life wherein we feel Torah's light,
    where we seek Your Presence,
a life where the inner questions of our heart
    will know response,
    and peace.
So may it be.

Vicki Hollander

We the collected bless the new moon.
We open ourselves to the new moon
as each week we open ourselves to the flame of the candle,
for measurement is a woman's,
of time, of the height of the flame,

of the passing of days.
We are earthy and lunar,
ordered by the calendar.
As you reflect upon the waters,
So our moods reflect you.

All creatures see her in the forest,
glinting on the waters,
lighting the city,
and the country road.
Their eyes gleam with her light.
Nocturnal creatures scurry in her path,
The seas are shimmering robes.
We meet where her light can shine upon us.
As we shine upon one another.

E. M. Broner

At the start of this month of soul searching and contemplation we should remember these wise words from the Mishnah: Rabbi Eliezer was wont to say – "Repent one day before your death".

Editors

Using *gematria*, the Hebrew word Elul has the same numerical value (67) as the word *binah* ('understanding'). Through understanding comes Teshuvah, as it is written (Isaiah 6:10): "and understanding with their heart, they return and are healed."

Siddur Rabbi Yaabetz

Traditionally we say Psalm 27 twice each day during the month of Elul in order to help us prepare ourselves inwardly for the coming of the Days of Awe.

One line in this Psalm seems strange. The Psalmist says: "*One* thing only do I ask of the Lord" and then he proceeds to ask for *two* things: that he may be able to *dwell* in the House of the Lord *and* that he may be able to *visit* God's holy place. *Which is it* that he wants – that he may be able to *dwell* there or that he may be able to *visit* there?

Rabbi Shlomo Riskin explains it this way: There are two kinds of people who come to the synagogue on the High Holy Days. Each has one great advantage and each has one great disadvantage. There are those who come regularly to synagogue. They know the words, the melodies, the order of the service: this is their advantage. But they have one great disadvantage. Because they have said the words so often, because they have come to synagogue so many times, the words have become familiar and there is no surprise for them in the service. They can say the words quickly and by heart and so they have a tendency to take them for granted. Those who come only a few times a year have one great disadvantage. They do not know the prayers. They stumble over the words and they are not familiar with the order of the service. But they have one great advantage that the regulars do not have. They are not bored or jaded by the prayers. For them, the words are fresh and new and the service is a new discovery.

Jack Riemer

The Eternal One is my light and my salvation,
whom should I fear:

The Eternal One is the strength of my life,
of whom shall I be afraid?

When those bent on evil draw near to slander me,
when foes threaten, they stumble and fall.

Though an army encamp against me, my heart will not
fear.

Though war be waged against me, my trust would still be
firm.

One thing only do I ask of God:
to dwell in the house of the Eternal One
all the days of my life,
to behold the beauty of the Eternal God,
and to seek God in the sanctuary.

For God shelters me in the tabernacle in times of trouble,
hides me in the hidden places, sets me high upon a rock.

And now my head is held high above my enemies who
surround me.

Therefore in God's tent will I offer sacrifices of exultation.
I will sing, I will play music with joy before God.

Eternal One, hear my voice when I call,
take pity on me and answer me.

Come, my heart has said, seek God's presence.
I will seek Your presence, Eternal One.

Do not hide Your face from me,
do not turn away Your servant in anger,
for You have been my help.

Do not cast me off or forsake me, O God my Saviour.

Even if my father and mother were to desert me, Eternal
　　God, You will care for me still.

Eternal God, teach me Your ways,
lead me in straight paths.

Do not deliver me to those who hate me,
to those who bear false witness against me and plan to do
　　me harm.

You have caused me to believe that I shall see the goodness
　　of the Eternal One in the land of the living.

Put your hope in the Eternal One,
be strong, let your heart take courage,
only wait for the Eternal One.

Psalm 27

(Psalm 27 is traditionally recited daily during the month of Elul)

2

Renewal

Each new day, new month and new year offers the possibility of a fresh start, of renewing our lives and our energies, our expectations and our hopes.

Why sayest thou, O Jacob,
And speakest, O Israel:
"My way is hid from the Lord,
And my right is passed over from my God"?
Hast thou not known? Hast thou not heard
That the everlasting God, the Lord,
The Creator of the ends of the earth,
Fainteth not, neither is weary?
His discernment is past searching out.
He giveth power to the faint;
And of him that hath no might He increaseth strength.
Even the youths shall faint and be weary,
And the young men shall utterly fall;
But they that wait for the Lord shall renew their strength;
They shall mount up with wings as eagles;
They shall run, and not be weary;
They shall walk, and not faint.

Isaiah 40.27–31

Teach me, my God, to pray
and to recite blessings for the mystery of the withered leaf no
less than for the splendour of the ripened fruit;

for freedom to see, to feel, to breathe, to know, to hope
– and to fail.

Instruct my lips to sing Your praise
when time renews itself each dawn and night,
that my today be not as yesterday,
nor any of my days become routine.

Leah Goldberg

Say to the House of Israel: You have been saying, "Because
our transgressions and sins weigh upon us, we waste away;
how can we survive?" Tell them: As I live, says the Eternal
God, I do not desire the death of the wicked, but that they
may turn from their way and live. Turn back, turn back
from your evil ways; for why should you choose to die, O
House of Israel?

Ezekiel 33.10–11

Rabbi Bunam taught:
"This is how we must interpret the first words in the
Scripture: 'In the beginning is God's creation of the heaven
and the earth.' For even now, the world is still in a state of
creation. When a craftsman makes a tool and it is finished,
it does not require him any longer. Not so with the world!
Day after day, instant after instant, the world requires the
renewal of the powers of the primordial word through
which it was created, and if the power of these powers were
withdrawn from it for a single moment, it would lapse into
tohu vavohu (i.e. chaos)."

Martin Buber

Ruler of the universe!
At our season of renewal,
We are turning, bending,
Viewing front and back.

Ruler of the universe!
At our season of revival,
We are uncovering, revealing,
Sweeping out.

Ruler of blessing,
We lean upon the Gate,
Testing the hinges,
Rubbing sharp edges.

Ruler of mercy,
We test our souls,
Rubbing fresh cloth over sorrow,
Binding away disappointment.

Called, called to the Gate,
We jostle, then quiet,
As memory and hope
Soothe us.

Standing, striving,
We empty our hearts' longing
Before You, Holy One,
Source of Life.

Debbie Perlman

Said the Bratzlaver: "No physician can heal unless he is well
acquainted with the physiology and anatomy of the body. In
the same way, no healer of those sick in soul can cure them
unless he thoroughly understands what particular spiritual
remedy will furnish solace and comfort to every particular

disease of the soul. He must know what the soul lacks before he can cure it. One man may be cured by reading ethical books; another, by practicing more hospitality; a third, by the reading of Psalms; a fourth, by engaging in profound learning; a fifth, by performing deeds of kindness; a sixth, by doing communal work."

Louis I. Newman

The last word has not been spoken,
the last sentence has not been written,
the final verdict is not in.
It is never too late
to change my mind,
my direction,
to say no to the past
and yes to the future,
to offer remorse,
to ask and give forgiveness.
It is never too late
to start over again,
to feel again
to love again
to hope again . . .

Harold M. Schulweis

3

Hope

Jewish history is replete with many setbacks, with a multitude of collective and personal disasters, yet we have never lost our capacity to hope for better times.

O give thanks
that spring will always come
to make the heart leap,
that your winter ear remembers
a summer song,
and autumn colours return
to the jaded eye.

O make song
for lucid air of morning,
bright blood's beating,
life's flow deep and swift,
a kingdom of joy and awe
for us to dwell in.

O be glad
for eye and tongue,
to see and taste
the common of our days.

Chaim Stern

When evil darkens our world, give us light.
When despair numbs our souls, give us hope.
When we stumble and fall, lift us up.
When doubts assail us, give us trust.

When nothing seems sure, give us faith.
When ideals fade, renew our vision.
When we lose our way, be our Guide,
That we may find serenity in Your presence, and purpose
   doing Your will.

John D. Rayner

Lord, we thank You for Your gift of hope, our strength in times of trouble. Beyond the injustice of our time, its cruelty and its wars, we look forward to a world at peace when men deal kindly with each other, and no-one is afraid. Every bad deed delays its coming, every good one brings it nearer. May our lives be Your witness, so that future generations bless us. May the day come, as the prophet taught, when "the sun of righteousness will rise with healing in its wings." Help us to pray for it, to wait for it, to work for it and to be worthy of it. Blessed are You Lord, the hope of Israel. Amen.

Forms of Prayer

O God
give me strength to forget
evils over and done,
history's falls and failings,
yesterday's frozen hope.
And give me strength to keep watch
for fair weather after a stormy day,
incense of flowers
and quiet waves.

HOPE

Give me strength to wait and time to hope:
until the last day
strength to keep watch and rejoice
as doves are hatched and babes are born,
as flowers bud and blossom
and visions break out and grow.
Give me strength,
O God.

Eliezer Bugatin

   Only the hopeful earn the glory,
For the future is theirs;
Those who stand unflinching against the mountain
Shall gain its summit.
   So hopes the river, running to the sea,
To fulfil its dreams in the crash of waters.
So longs the tree, branching skywards
At last to touch the palm of sun.
   Therefore we love dawn as promise of day,
The nightingale's love-song as longing for birth,
The flowing of springs as beat of dreams made real,
Streams cutting channels for rivers of the future
And never growing weary.
And all who join hands, trusting creation –
These are the companions of hope.
   Forge, then, the vision of days to come:
As the waves shape the rocky shore,
As the smith moulds white hot steel to his purpose,
Form dreams of faithfulness.
   Desolation will not leave the desert,
Until it leaves the heart.

David Rokeach

Hope

There are times when each of us is sick with the world
And life weighs upon us like a heavy boulder
We cannot imagine any good or happy thought
We sink further and deeper into the pit of our despair.

There are times when each of us feels sorely hurt
The very thing we loved the most has been taken away
We feel empty, we feel alone, we are afraid.

There are times when all justice has fled
We have been wronged, cheated, unfairly beaten down
How could life deal such iniquities?
Why must our burdens be so severe?

These are moments all human beings share
When their hearts sink and their minds
entertain the worst
Fears assail us all
We tremble and shake at problems facing us.

At these times a little voice from within us rouses us
Often waiting until we reach the very brink of despair
It tells us that we can indeed prevail
At first in nothing more than a whisper.

So soft at first that we can hardly hear it
But we listen and we begin to heed
"What's it saying to me?" we mutter
And we bend our ear to catch its faint remarks.

And it tells us what we need to hear
From the tragedy or crisis that we feel

HOPE

Our bodies are once more released
Our minds are turned to brighter thoughts.

This little voice abiding in each of us is – hope
It is not logical or even reasonable
It is our heart telling our head that we cannot surrender
For to give in to the trials of life is to let them win over us.

From a whisper hope grows slowly
First in a moderate tone and finally to a roar
It supersedes fear, sorrow, and even despair
It gives us the courage to try again.

"Pick yourself up," it demands
"Can't you see that tomorrow has better things in store."
And we begin to believe in ourselves, and we arise
To meet tomorrow a little stronger and more prepared.

"Try again! Try until you succeed," it shouts.
And we forget our failures, our losses and all the blows we
    were dealt
Hope offers us another chance to be what we dream
It insists that life is worthwhile and we are on the winning
    team.

Hope abides in each of us
Giving us the energy to survive
"Life is very good," it assures us
"Carry on with your work, and you will be blessed."

Carol Backman

O Lord, I set my hope on You;
   my God, in You I trust;
   may I not be disappointed,
   may my enemies not exult over me.
O let none who look to You be disappointed;
   let the faithless be disappointed, empty-handed.
Let me know Your paths, O Lord;
   teach me Your ways;
   guide me in Your true way and teach me,
   for You are God, my deliverer;
   it is You I look to at all times.

Psalm 25

4

Belief

The High Holy Days and the month of Elul are special times encouraging the search for a deeper knowledge of God.

There is a paradox about the High Holy Days which we don't often talk about because it is faintly embarrassing but which perhaps we *should* talk about. And it is this. On the one hand, people often say to me: "I am not very religious, you know." Sometimes they say it self-deprecatingly and apologetically, sometimes boastfully and with bravado, and sometimes merely because British etiquette dictates that one must never admit to taking anything seriously – except something *really* serious, like football or cricket!

When people say that they are not very religious, what do they mean? I suppose two things. First, that they are not sure whether, or with what degree of conviction, they believe in God. Secondly, that they don't much care for ritual, including the ritual of communal worship, which they find largely a waste of time and therefore mostly stay away from, just as people with only a slight interest in music wouldn't often go to a concert.

So what is true religion? It is fundamentally an attitude to reality; a response of the whole of our being – mind, heart and soul – to the world in which we are placed. It is a sense of awe and wonder, an apprehension of the mystery beyond the commonplace, that produces, if only in rare moments, a feeling of joy too deep to be communicated except in music, poetry or prayer. It is what Wordsworth tried to convey when he wrote (in "Lines composed a few miles above Tintern Abbey"):

And I have felt
A presence that disturbs me with the joy
Of elevated thoughts; a sense sublime
Of something far more deeply interfused,
Whose dwelling is the light of setting suns,
And the round ocean and the living air,
And the blue sky, and in the mind of man . . .

Are we religious in that sense? I *hope* we are, at least a little. I know some claim that they are not, and some are so blasé that they can look at a sunset and see nothing but refracted light. I think Albert Einstein knew better when he wrote: "The fairest thing we can experience is the mysterious. It is the fundamental emotion which stands at the cradle of true art and true science. One who knows it not, can no longer wonder, no longer feel amazement, is as good as dead, a snuffed out candle."

John D. Rayner

Let all who seek You rejoice and be glad in You,
and let those who love Your salvation say continually:
Let God be magnified.
But I am poor and needy;
hasten to me, O God, my help and my deliverer.
Eternal God, do not delay.

Psalm 70.5–6

Faith is the life-breath of religion. Frequently it is regarded as a form of knowledge that is not derived from the usual sources of observation and deduction, through rational analysis and demonstration, but comes to us through inward perception in the absence of all proof. While this view still has its defenders in Judaism, there is the strong tendency to regard faith not as opposed to reason but supplementary to it. Faith and reason are the two eyes of the soul through which we look upon reality. When either of them fails to function, our vision is distorted. Only when they are properly focused do they afford us a balanced view of reality.

Faith means steadfastness, hope, and courage. Its absence spells vacillation and anxiety. Faith is an anchor in the sea of uncertainty and trouble, delivering from the paralysis of fear, and liberating man's creative powers. In the religious sense, faith represents personal avowal of the values of religion: the purposefulness of life, the reality of God, and the rightness of His will; and speaks commitment to these truths, whether they be disclosed by reason, grasped by intuition, or delivered by tradition. Faith constitutes an affirmation of life.

Samuel S. Cohon

The Radziminer Rebbe said: We cross an ocean and are rescued from a shipwreck, so we give thanks to God. Should we not thank God if we cross without a mishap? I am cured of a dangerous illness and recite a thanksgiving blessing. Should I not give thanks when I am well and preserved from illness?

Hasidic

My thoughts awaken me with Thy name,
And set Thy mercies before me.

They teach me of the soul Thou hast formed,
Bound up within me; – it is wonderful in mine eyes!

And my heart seeth Thee and hath faith in Thee
As though it had stood by at Sinai.

I have sought Thee in my visions, and there passed
Thy glory by me, descending in Thy clouds.

My musings have roused me from my couch
To bless Thy glorious Name, O Lord.

Judah Halevi

Belief in God is more than a simple acceptance of the idea
that God exists. It involves a particular view of life, a belief
that there is a spiritual quality in human life and in the
universe – and a belief that this spiritual quality matters.

Israel I. Mattuck

I love the Lord, because He has heard
    my voice and my supplications.
Because He inclined his ear to me,
    therefore I will call on Him as long as I live.
Gracious is the Lord, and righteous;
    our God is merciful.
The Lord protects the simple;
    When I was brought low, He saved me.
Return, O my soul, to your rest,
    for the Lord has dealt bountifully with you.

Psalm 116.1–2, 5–7

5

Forgiveness

One of Judaism's most fundamental beliefs about this season is that we will not be forgiven by God unless we have first sought forgiveness from those we have wronged.

The most beautiful thing that one can do is to forgive a wrong.

Eleazar ben Judah of Worms

If someone who has wronged you asks for your forgiveness you should not refuse it. As long as you are forgiving to others you will find forgiveness yourself.

Midrash

Uncertain of our ways, we look
to You. Remember Your compassion and
Your steadfast love, Eternal One, for they
are everlasting.

For You alone we wait in hope;
extend to us Your grace. Let not past errors
be held against us; when our merits are few,
let Your compassion be quick to meet us.

Seder Rav Amram

O God of forgiveness, I hereby forgive all those who have hurt me, all those who have wounded me whether deliberate or inadvertent, whether by word or by deed. May no one be punished on my account. As I forgive and pardon those who have wronged me may those whom I have hurt forgive and pardon me whether I acted deliberately or inadvertently, whether by word or by deed.

Editors

Will days indeed come with their gift of forgiveness and
    blessing
And then, with a light heart and mind as a wayfarer goes,
You'll walk in the field, with the clover-leaves gently caressing
Your bare feet and stubble deliciously stinging your toes?

Or rain overtake you, its throng of drops beating aloud
On your bare, fragrant head, on your neck, on your
    shoulders and chest,
And will there expand in you, as in the skirts of a cloud,
A sunlight of quiet and rest?

And breathing the smell of the furrow that lies over yonder
You'll see the sun's rays in the puddle, a mirror of gold.
And things are so simple, alive, and a pleasure to fondle,
To love and to hold.

Alone you will walk there, unscorched by the fires, nor stumble
On highways that bristle with horror and blood; and again
In pureness' embrace you shall be meek and humble
As a blade of grass, as mere man.

Leah Goldberg

A rebuke is a gift and a challenge. Without our friends, colleagues, and families being willing to point out our own errors of judgment or action, we bind ourselves to our own faults. Their courage to articulate disappointment in our actions is an indispensable prerequisite to self-improvement and refinement.

We cannot afford to wait for the perfect, loving hero to inform us of our flaws. Instead, we rely on those around us to act as our early warning systems, pointing out moral failure and ethical obtuseness before it's too late to improve. And when they do, we must be able to really listen.

Bradley Shavit Artson

Observe, then, how compulsion shackles me,
From toils of mine own twisting, set me free.
Forgive my sin: pardoning, set aside
My trespasses, and overlook my pride.
But, if I merit lack, and Thou dost spurn
(Perish the thought) my self-abased return,
If turmoil, caused by my offence, the sound
Of this mine own petition's voice has drowned,
I say, never will God despise the prayer
Of innocent folk: do Thou, therefore, spare
This holy congregation, as they all
Pour forth their supplication, great and small,
And sacrificial bulls replace with sighs
And plaints that out their lips towards Thee rise,
Each one his sins confessing, in this wise:

Raphael Loewe

6

Holy Life

In Judaism a holy life is not necessarily one spent in prayer, meditation and fasting, but in doing good deeds, showing compassion to others, and actively helping those in need.

All the month of Elul before eating and sleeping we should sit and look into our souls, and search our deeds, that we may make confession.

Maharil

If you always assume
the one sitting next to you
is the Messiah
waiting for some simple human kindness

You will soon come to weigh your words
and watch your hands.

And if the Messiah chooses
not to be revealed
in your time –

It will not matter.

Danny Siegel

In the world to come, all will be asked: "What was your occupation?" If they reply, "We fed the hungry," they will be told: "This is the gate of the Eternal One; let those who fed the hungry enter." If they reply, "We gave drink to the thirsty," they will be told: "This is the gate of the Eternal One; let those who gave drink to the thirsty enter." If they reply, "We clothed the naked," they will be told: "This is the gate of the Eternal One; let those who clothed the naked enter." So, too, with those who raised orphans, gave charity, and performed deeds of kindness.

Midrash

The worshipper must direct his heart to each word that he utters. He is like a man who walks through a garden collecting rare and precious flowers, plucking them one by one in order to weave a garland. So we move from word to word and from page to page combining the words into prayers. Each word seizes hold of us and cleaves to us; it entreats us not to abandon it, saying, "Consider my light, notice my grace. Be careful as you take hold of me, take care as you pronounce my name."

Nachman of Bratzlav

The rewards for doing *mitzvot* are not quoted in the Torah, so that one does not concentrate only on important religious duties and neglect seemingly minor ones. This has been compared to a king instructing his servants to plant all sorts of beautiful trees in his park, but not letting them know how much he would pay them for each kind of tree. If he had done so they would have concentrated on planting only the trees for which they would have received the most money.

So it is with *mitzvot*. God has given us many religious duties and instructed us to perform as many as possible.

Levi Gersonides

We reflect upon all the evils and the mischief, the waste, the cruelties, and the follies, the hair-splitting, the casuistry, and the formalism, the hypocrisy, the intolerance, and the aridity, which the divorce of religion from morality has produced in almost every creed. The good man, we say, be his belief or unbelief what it may, is not far from God. He possesses the root of the matter. Religion is righteousness; or, it is righteousness touched by emotion; it is purity and sanctity of life. It is not dogma; it is not belief; it is not ceremonies and observances; but it is goodness and justice; it is righteousness; it is love.

Claude G. Montefiore

A psalm of David when he was in the wilderness of Judah
O God, You are my God, I seek You,
   my soul thirsts for You;
my flesh faints for You,
   as in a dry and weary land where
   there is no water.
So I have looked upon You in the sanctuary
   beholding Your power and glory.
Because Your steadfast love is better than life,
   my lips will praise You.
So I will bless You as long as I live;
   I will lift up my hands and call on Your name.
My soul is satisfied as with a rich feast
   and my mouth praises You with joyful lips
when I think of You on my bed,

and meditate on You in the watches of the night;
for You have been my help,
    and in the shadow of Your wings I sing for joy.
My soul clings to You;
    Your right hand upholds me.

Psalm 63.1–8

7

Divine Presence

Those who experience the *shechinah*, God's immediate and consoling presence in their lives, are touched by a special blessing. The faith that God dwells in and around us is one of the most comforting beliefs of rabbinic Judaism.

Shechinah Mekor Chayyeynu –
Divine Presence, Source of our lives, shelter us under the wings of Your compassion.

Machzor Ruach Chadashah

On Being a Woman in Shul

Judaism is a man's religion not only in substance and in practice but in its symbolic theology. God is male. Israel in relation to God is female: the bridegroom God and the Virgin Israel. The Shechinah, the Divine Presence, represents the female potency within God. The Torah is female, the Sabbath is female. In relation to them, God is male. In the books of the Prophets and, of course, in the Song of Songs, marriage and sexual relations symbolise the ties between God and Israel, Israel and the Sabbath, Israel and Torah.

Lucy S. Dawidowicz

Shechinah is the indwelling presence of God in this world. It is the divinity we may experience when enthralled by the beauties of nature, in deep encounter with another human being (*neshamah*) or alone in moments of stillness, whenever the heart is open. Judaism claims that this encounter may also take place in the context of sacred study ("Two who are together and study torah, *shechinah* abides in their midst") and that it also has a moral dimension: *shechinah* is to be found in human acts of justice and compassion.

Kabbalistic tradition sees *shechinah* as the tenth of the *sefirot*, the link between the hidden God and lower worlds. In Kabbalistic writings, especially those stemming from the *Zohar*, *shechinah* is described primarily in feminine terms, as the bride of the blessed Holy One and the Queen of the universe. Their sacred marital union (which is in fact a reunion, since they are originally one) becomes the goal of all religious life. As Kabbalists perform the commandments they dedicate their actions to "the union of blessed Holy One and His *shechinah*, in love and fear, in the name of all Israel." The reunion of "male" and "female" within the God-head is understood as the restoration of harmony to the entire universe, allowing the flow of Divine Presence to become fully manifest throughout the world.

Arthur Green

"Where is the dwelling of God?"
This was the question with which the Rabbi of Kotzk surprised a number of learned men who happened to be visiting him. They laughed at him: "What a thing to ask! Is not the whole world full of His glory?"
Then he answered his own question:
"God dwells where man lets Him in."

Martin Buber

O God, You are near as the very air we breathe and the light around us; yet our thought's uttermost reach falls short of You, and we often feel that You are far from us. We want to reach You, but cannot. We seek the light and warmth of Your presence, as a plant turns to the sun, but our hearts are chilled. Though You are near, we feel lonely.

O make our desire for You so strong that it will hold in itself the power of fulfilment! Let Your light penetrate our dull vision, to reveal to us the glory and joy of Your eternal presence.

As the swimmer gives himself to the sea, as the bird gives itself to the air, as all life gives itself to life, so may we give ourselves to You, our God.

Israel I. Mattuck

For me, encountering God has meant addressing God directly in my own words and seeking a direct reply in any form describable as divine revelation – God becoming manifest to humans. However, establishing such a connection is almost impossibly difficult, not necessarily because God is inaccessible – quite the contrary – but because I am. I hesitate to make the approach, feeling unworthy, daunted by the prospect of absolute vulnerability, unprepared no matter when it is, fearful of raw unmediated truth, and, absurdly, embarrassed by the lack of parity between me and the One I am about to address.

Arlene Agus

DIVINE PRESENCE

You who live in the shelter of the Most High,
  who abide in the shadow of the Almighty,
will say to the Lord, "My refuge and my fortress;
  my God in whom I trust."
For he will deliver you from the snare of the fowler
  and from the deadly pestilence;
he will cover you with his pinions,
  and under his wings you will find refuge;
  his faithfulness is a shield and buckler.
You will not fear the terror of the night,
  or the arrow that flies by day,
or the pestilence that stalks in the darkness,
  or the destruction that wastes at noonday.

Psalm 91.1–6

8

Doubt

Without doubt, faith cannot be tested and strengthened. The struggle to overcome doubt is a challenge to all who search for a deeper faith.

I have no idea to whom,
I have no idea for what I am praying.
A prayer is bound up within me
and searches for a God
and searches for a Name.
I pray in the countryside
in the roar of the city street
together with the wind which rushes before me.
A prayer is bound up within me
and searches for a God,
and searches for a Name.

Kadya Molodowsky

The Sassover Rebbe taught: Nothing is altogether without its value. Error may lead to truth, lack of faith may lead to God.

For if someone comes to you asking for help, you must not refuse, saying: "Have faith; God will help." No, act as if there were no God, and none to help but you.

Chaim Stern

A disciple asked the Baal Shem: "Why is it that one who clings to God and knows he is close to Him, sometimes experiences a sense of interruption and remoteness?"

The Baal Shem explained: "When a father sets out to teach his little son to walk, he stands in front of him and holds his two hands on either side of the child, so that he cannot fall, and the boy goes toward his father between his father's hands. But the moment he is close to his father, he moves away a little, and holds his hands further apart, and he does this over and over, so that the child may learn to walk."

Martin Buber

Resistance to the word of God is no monopoly of the modern mind. Men and women have always been impelled to reject it, as the Bible itself bears striking witness. And in rejecting it they have always employed arguments and justifications that have seemed conclusive in terms of the culture of the time.

The fact of the matter seems to be that the modern unbeliever refuses to believe for the same basic reason that the unbelievers of all ages have refused: the biblical word is a decisive challenge to their pretensions of self-sufficiency and to all the strategies that they have devised to sustain them. Modern men and women are ready to 'accept' revelation if that revelation is identified with their own intellectual discovery or poetical intuition. But with the revelation that comes from beyond to shatter their self-sufficiency, to expose the dereliction of their life and to call them to a radical transformation of heart, with that revelation they will have nothing to do.

Will Herberg

I find it is Yom Kippur,
                  and here I am
Down by the river
                  in late afternoon.
There is a poem
                  I have read
In several versions,
                  about the Jewish writer
Who doesn't fast, who
                  doesn't go to synagogue
On Yom Kippur,
                  the day of atonement,
And here is my construction
                  of that poem.
Here am I,
             on the embankment
Staring at the river,
                  while the lights
Are coming up,
                  signifying darkness, the end of the fast,
Though it's not over yet,
                  and the congregations,
Are still gathered
                  in the synagogues,
Praying, *slach lonu, m'chal lonu*,
                  forgive us, pardon us,
We have sinned,
                  we deserve punishment,
We are like clay,
                  in the hands of the great Potter,
Who has shaped us all,
                  even, you could say, me
Here by the river,
                  watching the water

DOUBT

And the rubbish
                drifting on the water,
Imagining what is
                swaying in under the bridges,
Is something of exile,
                formless but perceptible,
Bringing in the names
                of pious cities
Vilna and Minsk and Vitebsk
                            (my own ancestral names)
And vanished communities,
                behind curtains
Of forgetfulness,
                And ordinary human change,
Praying communities
                on Yom Kippur and other days
Clinging to and turning from,
                        that which I cling to
And turn from,
                if you like the covenant
That keeps me fasting,
                but not in synagogue
Today, Yom Kippur.
                I go into the gardens
Sit down on a bench,
                read my newspaper,
And wait
        for the first star.

Arthur C. Jacobs

The difficulty for us in this process of atonement is to be truly sincere about our repentance. This is excessively hard. In the Vidui (confession) on the Day of Atonement we do express in words our regret "for the sins which we have committed against Thee willingly or by compulsion, openly or secretly, presumptuously or unwittingly . . ." But words alone are not repentance. I have already said that we are in danger of losing entirely that sense of sin which moved our forefathers. We are no longer afraid or superstitious as they were. We know – though, to be sure, not always – that we are doing, or have done, wrong. Certainly education is the way of progress; yet the Rabbis tell us: "He in whom wisdom comes before the fear of sin, his wisdom will not endure." What is meant is that the fear of sin is all-important, and no knowledge or intellectual reasoning can make up for it.

How then shall we feel true regret for our sins? I think the best way is to steep ourselves in the wonderful liturgy of this Day, to lay ourselves open to the appeal of the unique calls to repentance felt and expressed by the greatest teachers of the past.

Vivian Simmons

I do not know how to ask You, Lord of the world, and even if I did know, I could not bear to do it. How could I venture to ask You why everything happens as it does, why we are driven from one exile into another, why our foes are allowed to torment us so. But in the Haggadah, the father of him "who does not know how to ask" is told: "It is for you to disclose it to him." And, Lord of the world, am I not Your son? I do not ask you to reveal to me the secret of Your ways – I could not bear it! But show me one thing: show me what this very moment means to me, what it demands of me, what You, Lord, are telling me through my life at this moment. O I do not ask You to tell me *why* I suffer, but only whether I suffer for Your sake!

Levi Yitzchak of Berditchev

9

Nature

In Elul the summer days are coming to an end yet the natural world remains full of colour and fruitfulness; those who truly open their eyes will see God's bounty all around them.

In the beginning, You made a simple world
day and night, water and earth, plants and animals.

But now You create galaxies beyond systems
in the unending curve of space.

Now we know You create with subtlety
the invisible atom with its secret heart of power.

You create with delicacy, with violence,
the cell splitting, becoming life.

Filled with joy, You make a human being
a whole world, mysterious, delicate, violent.

Overflowing with joy, You create myriads of people,
fling galaxies across space, sow them with countless kinds
    of life.

Your love, massive, cosmic, joyful, explodes around us, as in
the beginning, in a burst of light, a rush of waters, in the cry
of birth, in ourselves, even in ourselves.

Ruth F. Brin

Master of the Universe,
grant me the ability to be alone;
may it be my custom to go outdoors each day
among the trees and grass, among all
growing things,
and there may I be alone and enter into prayer,
to talk with the One that I belong to.
May I express there everything in my heart,
and may all the foliage of the field
(all grasses, trees and plants)
may they all awake at my coming,
to send the powers of their life into the
words of my prayer
so that my prayer and speech are made whole
through the life and spirit of all growing things,
which are made as one by their
transcendent Source.

Nachman of Bratzlav

Who made the world:
Who made the swan and the black bear?
Who made the grasshopper?
The grasshopper, I mean –
the one who has flung herself out of the grass
the one who is eating sugar out of my hand,
who is moving her jaws back and forth instead of up and
    down –
who is gazing around with her enormous and complicated
    eyes.
Now she lifts her pale forearms and thoroughly washes her
    face.
Now she snaps her wings open, and floats away.

I don't know exactly what a prayer is.
I do know how to pay attention, how to fall down
into the grass, how to kneel down in the grass,
how to be idle and blessed, how to stroll through the fields,
which is what I have been doing all day.
Tell me, what else should I have done?
Doesn't everything die at last, and too soon?
Tell me, what is it you plan to do
with your one wild and precious life?

Mary Oliver

Summer's Elegy

Day after day, day after still day,
The summer has begun to pass away.
Starlings at twilight fly clustered and call,
And branches bend, and leaves begin to fall.
The meadow and the orchard grass are mown,
And the meadowlark's house is cut down.

The little lantern bugs have doused their fires,
The swallows sit in rows along the wires.
Berry and grape appear among the flowers
Tangled against the wall in secret bowers,
And cricket now begins to hum the hours
Remaining to the passion's slow procession
Down from the high place and the golden session
Wherein the sun was sacrificed for us.
A failing light, no longer numinous,
Now frames the long and solemn afternoons
Where butterflies regret their closed cocoons.
We reach the place unripe, and made to know
As with a sudden knowledge that we go
Away forever, all hope of return

Cut off, hearing the crackle of the burning blade behind us, and the terminal sound
Of apples dropping on the dry ground.

Howard Nemerov

Beauty

I shall never agree
That the beauty of things on the surface we see.
I shall always seek it in the mists and the shadows hidden,
Under the veil of mystery, under the lock of the forbidden,
In crevices of rocks, in fear of the pit.
With rich thoughts the depths I shall pierce and split
Till the farthest atoms that God concealed
Will as images be to me revealed.
I shall strain my eyes and sharpen my ears
On the lips of stammerers and children in tears,
Where is the primal source of colour and tonality.
I like to believe that the rainbow we see
On the other side of heaven a thousand times lovelier
    must be.

Alter Esselin

Rabbi Nachman of Bratzlav

The grasses in the field shook happily
When Rabbi Nachman of Bratzlav came quietly,
Telling his marvellous tales of what he had heard and seen,
And his prayers bearing leafage fresh and green.

The birds hovered over him, lost in thought,
Hearing the songs of mystery he brought.
At night the woods were full of peacefully sleeping birds,
Lulled to rest by the magic of his words.

And all insects and worms that fly and crawl,
All inanimate things, rocks and sands, great and small,
Listened to Rabbi Nachman of Bratzlav as he passed on his
way,
And repeated the words they heard him say.

Rabbi Nachman knew their speech, and he could hear,
And what they said was like a song to his ear,
He spoke to them and told them his marvellous tales
Of coming days and hope that never fails.

Aleph Katz

Praise the Eternal One, O my soul! O God, You are very
great!

You are arrayed in glory and majesty.

You wrap Yourself in light as with a garment. You stretch
out the heavens like a curtain.

The clouds are Your chariot. You ride on the wings of the
wind.

You make the winds Your messengers, and flames of fire
Your ministers.

You set the earth on its foundations, that it might never be
moved.

You send streams to spring forth in the valleys; they run
between the mountains,

Giving drink to the beasts of the field, quenching the thirst
of the wild asses.

The birds of the air nest on their banks, and sing among the leaves.

You make grass grow for the cattle, and plants for people to cultivate,

That bread may come forth from the earth, and wine to cheer the heart.

You made the moon to mark the seasons; the sun knows its time of setting.

You make darkness, and it is night, when all the beasts go prowling.

Young lions roar for prey, demanding their food from God.

When the sun rises, they slink away, and go to their lairs for rest.

Then men and women go to their work, to their toil until evening.

How manifold are Your works, Eternal One! In wisdom You have made them all; the earth is full of Your creations.

Let Your glory endure for ever; rejoice, O God, in Your works.

I will sing to the Eternal One all my days; I will sing praises to my God as long as I live.

from Psalm 104

10

God

The search for God is at the very heart of the High Holy Days, yet God may be found at any moment. When we pray to God for forgiveness, if only in a whisper, we believe that we shall be heard.

Said Rabbi Levi: "God appears to Israel like a mirror in which many faces can be reflected; a thousand people look at it, it looks at each of them."

Midrash

When men were children, they thought of God as a father;
When men were slaves, they thought of God as a master;
When men were subjects, they thought of God as a king.
But I am a woman, not a slave, not a subject,
not a child who longs for God as father or mother.
I might imagine God as teacher or friend, but those images,
like king, master, father or mother, are too small for me
    now.
God is the force of motion and light in the universe;
God is the strength of life on our planet;
God is the power moving us to do good;
God is the source of love springing up in us.
God is far beyond what we can comprehend.

Ruth F. Brin

Our ancestors acclaimed the God
Whose handiwork they read
In the mysterious heavens above,
And in the varied scene of earth below,
In the orderly march of days and nights,
Of seasons and years,
And in the chequered fate of humankind.

Night reveals the limitless caverns of space,
Hidden by the light of day,
And unfolds horizonless vistas
Far beyond imagination's ken.
The mind is staggered,
Yet soon regains its poise,
And peering through the boundless dark,
Orients itself anew by the light of distant suns
Shrunk to glittering sparks.
The soul is faint, yet soon revives,
And learns to spell once more the name of God
Across the newly-visioned firmament.

Lift your eyes, look up; who made these stars?

God is the oneness
That spans the fathomless deeps of space
And the measureless eons of time,
Binding them together in deed, as we do in thought.

God is the sameness
In the elemental substance of stars and planets,
Of this our earthly abode and of all that it holds.

God is the unity of all that is,
The uniformity of all that moves,
The rhythm of all things
And the nature of their interaction.

GOD

God is the mystery of life,
Enkindling inert matter with inner drive and purpose.

God is the creative flame
That transfigures lifeless substance,
Leaping into ever higher realms of being,
Brightening into the radiant glow of feeling,
till it runs into the white fire of thought.

And though no sign of living things
Breaks the eternal silence of the spheres,
We cannot deem this earth,
This tiny speck in the infinitude,
Alone instinct with God.

By that token which unites the worlds in bonds of matter
Are all the worlds bound in the bond of Life.

God is in the faith
By which we overcome the fear of loneliness,
Of helplessness, of failure and of death.

God is in the hope
Which, like a shaft of light,
Cleaves the dark abysms
Of sin, of suffering, and of despair.

God is in the love
Which creates, protects, forgives.

It is God's spirit
That broods upon the chaos we have wrought,
Disturbing its static wrongs,
And stirring into life the formless beginnings
Of the new and better world.

Mordecai M. Kaplan

Our God
in heaven and on earth, mighty and revered,
one among millions, whose word is power,
whose command creates, whose fame is eternal,
who lives forever, who sees everything,
enthroned in mystery, crowned with deliverance,
robed in righteousness, cloaked in zeal,
girded with justice, equity His shelter,
faithfulness His counsel, truth His work,
righteous and just, near to those calling in truth,
lofty and exalted, abiding in the heavens.

He suspends the earth in space;
He lives, awesome, exalted and holy.

Eleazer Kallir

Consider how high God is above the world, yet if anyone
goes into a synagogue and stands behind a pillar and prays
in a whisper, the Holy One, ever to be praised, listens to
their prayer . . . can there be a God nearer than this, who is
as near to us as the mouth is to the ear?

Talmud

Praise Me, says God, and I will know that you love Me.
Curse Me, says God, and I will know that you love Me.
Praise Me or curse Me,
And I will know that you love Me.

Sing out My graces, says God.
Raise your fist against Me and revile, says God.
Sing out graces or revile,
Reviling is also a kind of praise, says God.

But if you sit fenced off in your apathy, says God,
If you sit entrenched in, "I don't give a hang", says God,

GOD

If you look at the stars and yawn,
If you see suffering and don't cry out,
If you don't praise and you don't revile,
Then I created you in vain, says God.

Aaron Zeitlin

O, Thou my God: all
   peoples Praise Thee and
   assure Thee of their
   devotion.
But what does it mean to
   Thee whether I do this or
   not?

Who am I that I should
   believe my prayers are
   necessary?
When I say 'God', I know
   that I speak of the Only,
   Eternal, Omnipotent,
   All-Knowing and
   Inconceivable One, of
   whom I neither can nor
   should make for myself
   an image; on whom I
   neither may nor can make
   any demand, who will
   fulfil my most fervent
   prayer or ignore it.

O, Du mein Gott: alle
   Völker Preisen Dich und
   versichern Dich ihrer
   Ergebenheit.
Was aber kann es Dir
   bedeuten, Ob ich das
   auch tue oder nicht?

Wer bin ich, dass ich
   glauben soll, mein Gebet
   sei eine Notwendigkeit?
Wenn ich Gott sage, weiss
   ich, dass ich damit von
   dem Einzigen, Ewigen,
   Allmächtigen,
   Allwissenden und
   Unvorstellbaren spreche,
   von dem ich mir ein Bild
   weder machen kann
   noch soll. An den ich
   keinen Anspruch erheben
   kann oder soll, der mein
   heissestes Gebet erfüllen
   oder nicht beachten wird.

And yet I pray, as each one
   prays who is alive; and
   yet I pray for mercies,
   miracles, fulfilments.

And yet I pray, for I do
   not want to lose the
   blissful feeling of unity, of
   communion with Thee.
O Thou, my God: Thy
   mercy left us prayer as
   a bond, a blissful bond
   with Thee: a gift greater
   than any fulfilment.

Und trotzdem bete ich,
   wie alles Lebende betet;
   trotzdem erbitte ich
   Gnaden und Wunder,
   Erfüllungen.

Trotzdem bete ich, denn
   ich will nicht des
   beseligenden Gefühls der
   Einigkeit, der Vereinigung
   mit Dir, verlustig werden.
O Du mein Gott, Deine
   Gnade hat uns das
   Gebet gelassen, als eine
   Verbindung mit Dir.
   Als eine Seligkeit, die
   uns mehr gibt, als jede
   Erfüllung.

Arnold Schoenberg

II

Prayer

The High Holy Days and the days which precede them are filled with prayer – our challenge is to let the prayers we utter bring purpose and direction to our lives.

The Holy One said to the Jews: "I have said to you – when you pray, pray in the synagogue in your city. If you cannot pray in the synagogue, pray in your field. If you cannot pray in your field, pray in your house. And if you cannot pray in your house, pray on your bed. And if you cannot pray on your bed, reflect in your heart."

Midrash

When, in times of need and danger one is unable to muster the requisite concentration and devotion for the daily Prayer, a brief alternative may be substituted.

Rabbi Eliezer suggests:
   Do Your Will in heaven above,
   and grant calmness of spirit
   to those who revere You on earth below;
   and do what seems good in Your sight.
   Blessed are You Eternal, who hears prayer.

The Sages suggest:

Israel's needs are many and their knowledge is limited. May it be Your Will, Eternal God, that you give to each one of them according to their needs and grant to each what they lack. Blessed are You Eternal, who hears prayers.

Talmud

How do I learn to pray? There is really only one answer: pray! Pray other people's prayers. You will appropriate them to yourself by using them and pouring your own personality into them. Do not wait until you 'feel like' praying, or until you know how to pray. You never will.

Steven S. Schwarzschild

Normally, we are compelled to pass from one task to another in quick succession; one duty is completed to be followed immediately by the next; a difficulty surmounted, a problem solved is replaced with such rapidity by further worries and by other cares that we have no choice, in daily life, but to live from one minute to another, to eliminate from our minds everything but that which is immediately ahead of us and which demands immediate attention.

In worship, however, we are freed from the pressure of life. There are no immediate tasks to be performed: no insistent needs clamouring for immediate satisfaction. For once, we are guaranteed Time and Quietude – the rarest possessions in life today. For once, we can escape from the tyranny of the next minute with its worries, tasks and duties.

Leslie I. Edgar

PRAYER

I have always found prayer difficult. So often it seems like a fruitless game of hide-and-seek where we seek and God hides . . . Yet I cannot leave prayer alone for long. My need drives me to God. And I have a feeling that . . . finally all my seeking will prove infinitely worthwhile. And I am not sure what I mean by "finding". Some days my very seeking seems a kind of "finding". And, of course, if "finding" means the end of "seeking", it were better to go on seeking.

Israel I. Mattuck

Our Father, our King, give us again
A sense of wonder at Your creation,
At the myriad of suns, the silent moon,
The gentle rain, and the ferocious sea.
Make us humble enough to thank You
When we see the grass grow.

Our Father, our King, give us again
A belief in man, in his courage and strength,
His power to love, his will for peace.
Make us sensitive enough to feel
Your divine image there
Even when he blasphemes.

Our Father, our King, give us again
A faith in Israel, in the prophetic marrow
Of our bones, that Your truth may be seen
In our stance among nations.
Make us strong enough to reject
The call "to be like the others".

Our Father, our King, give us again
A passion for silence, that from within
We may shut out the world
And hear Your quiet, insistent voice.

Make us wise enough not to utter
An instant opinion.

Our King, give us again the subject's abasement
Before his Sovereign, powerful yet forgiving.
Our Father, give us again the trust of the child
Who knows his father, and is comforted.

David Goldstein

Hear our voice, Eternal One our God; have compassion upon us, and accept our prayer with favour and mercy.

Help us to return to You, O God; then we shall return. Renew our days as in the past.

Siddur Lev Chadash

12

Reconciliation

Getting closer to God might be the religious person's dream, but getting closer to our fellow men and women, especially those from whom we are estranged, is the prize that may, in its winning, bring us closer to a realization of God's presence in our lives.

The Tzanzer Rebbe used to tell this story about himself: "In my youth, when I was fired with the love of God, I thought I would convert the whole world to God. But soon I discovered that it would be quite enough to convert the people who lived in my town, and I tried for a long time, but I did not succeed. Then I realised that my programme was still much too ambitious, and I concentrated on the persons in my own household. But I could not convert them either. Finally it dawned on me: I must work upon myself, so that I may give true service to God. But I did not accomplish even this."

Martin Buber

Bear in mind that life is short, and that with every passing day you are nearer to the end of your life. Hence how can you waste your time on petty quarrels and family discords?

Restrain your anger; hold your temper in check, and enjoy peace with everyone.

Nachman of Bratzlav

For transgressions between ourselves and God, the Day of Atonement atones; but for transgressions between one human being and another, the Day of Atonement does not atone unless they have reconciled one another.

Mishnah

Our agony is that we are capable of acts which contradict God's great expectations of us. Our glory is that we are capable of achieving atonement and reconciliation.

Moses Maimonides

The Rabbi of Lelov said to his Hasidim:
"A man cannot be redeemed until he recognises the flaws in his soul and tries to mend them. A nation cannot be redeemed until it recognises the flaws in its soul and tries to mend them. Whoever permits no recognition of his flaws, be it man or nation, permits no redemption. We can be redeemed to the extent to which we recognise ourselves.

"When Jacob's sons said to Joseph: 'We are upright men,' he answered: 'That is why I spoke unto you saying: You are spies.' But later, when they confessed the truth with their lips and with their hearts, and said to one another, 'We are verily guilty concerning our brother,' the first gleam of their redemption dawned. Overcome with compassion, Joseph turned aside and wept."

Martin Buber

RECONCILIATION

When two people had quarrelled, Aaron would go and sit
with one of them and say: My child, do you realise what your
neighbour is doing? He is tormenting himself and tearing his
clothes and saying: 'I am so ashamed that I offended him!'
And Aaron would sit with him until he had drained all anger
out of his heart. Then Aaron would go and do the same to
the other man. Later when the two met, they would embrace
and kiss each other.

Talmud

Shame-stricken, bending low,
My God, I come before Thee, for I know
That even as Thou on high
Exalted art in power and majesty,
So weak and frail am I,
That perfect as Thou art,
So I deficient am in every part.

Thou art all-wise, all-good, all-great, divine
Yea, Thou art God: eternity is Thine,
While I, a thing of clay,
The creature of a day,
Pass shadowlike, a breath, that comes and flees away . . .

My God, I know that my sins are numberless,
More than I can recall to memory
Or tell their tale: yet some will I confess,
Even a few, though as a drop it be
In all the sea.

I will declare my trespasses and sin
And peradventure silence then may fall
Upon their waves and billows' raging din,
And Thou wilt hear from heaven, when I call,
And pardon all . . .

Solomon ibn Gabirol

13

The Journey

The journey of life can be mystically epitomized by these days of repentance, which at their conclusion point us towards renewed life.

If you have no past you have no future either, you are a foundling in this world, with no father or mother, without tradition, without duties to what comes after you, the future, the eternal. If you service only yourself, you measure and weigh everything against yourself – there is nothing for you to strive towards. You have moods, but no character; desires, but no will – no great love, no great hate – you [merely] flirt with life.

I. L. Peretz

A Prayer
Let me do my work each day;
and if the darkened hours
of despair overcome me, may I
not forget the strength
that comforted me in the
desolation of other times. May I
still remember the bright
hours that found me walking
over the silent hills of my
childhood, or dreaming on the

margin of the quiet river,
when a light glowed within me,
and I promised my early God
to have courage amid the
tempests of the changing years.
Spare me from bitterness
and from the sharp passions of
unguarded moments. May
I not forget that poverty and
riches are of the spirit.
Though the world know me not,
may my thoughts and actions
be such as shall keep me friendly
with myself. Lift my eyes
from the earth, and let me not
forget the uses of the stars.
Forbid that I should judge others
lest I condemn myself.
Let me not follow the clamour of
the world, but walk calmly
in my path. Give me a few friends
who will love me for what
I am; and keep ever burning
before my vagrant steps
the kindly light of hope. And
though age and infirmity overtake
me, and I come not within
sight of the castle of my dreams,
teach me still to be thankful
for life, and for time's olden
memories that are good and
sweet; and may the evening's
twilight find me gentle still.

Max Ehrmann

Let me not swerve from my life's path,
Let not my spirit wither and shrivel
In its thirst for You
And lose the dew
With which You sprinkled it
When I was young.

May my heart be open
To every broken soul,
To orphaned life,
To every stumbler
Wandering unknown
And groping in the shadow.

Bless my eyes, purify me to see
Man's beauty rise in the world.

Deepen and broaden my senses
To absorb a fresh
Green, flowering world,
To take from it the secret
Of blossoming in silence.

Grant strength to yield fine fruits,
Quintessence of my life,
Steeped in my very being,
Without expectation of reward.

And when my time comes –
Let me slip into the night
Demanding nothing, God, of man,
Or of You.

Hillel Bavli

Psalm

There are a very few moments when you
Lift your soul within you like a drop of crystal.
The world is filled with its sun and broken colours,
Collection of sights and trembling objects,
And you perceive the world
As the drop of crystal.
Yet your world strains quivering to pour out,
Not to remain full,
Towards all limits, quivers.
You are given to all worlds.
The ends of stretches of air flow from your eyes,
Fears of darkness crouch in them,
Distant and close things find you
And demand your soul.

Stand, in night's silence,
On mountain summits,
Among the big cold stars lift your head.
The lives below you sink to the ground,
On the last burning of their grief
A black oblivion comes down.
You, though, wake to terrors
Above the darkness.
If a star drops
Through fear of the flamed roar
Rising from the distress of oblivion to the sky
It falls in the depths of your soul
And is consumed.

In the coming of morning
You are hovering over the face of the deep,
Drawing over it your profound heaven
With the great sun in your hands
Till evening.

Abraham Ben Yitzchak

So many people go through life filling the storeroom of their minds with odds and ends of a grudge here, a jealousy there, a pettiness, a selfishness – all ignoble. Our true task is to create a noble memory, a mind filled with grandeur, forgiveness, restless ideals, and the dynamic ethical ferment preached by all religions at their best.

Leo Baeck

Is it really the end? The path is still clear.
The mists of life still beckon from afar
The sky is still blue, the grass green;
Autumn is coming.

I shall accept the judgment. My heart harbours no
   complaint.
How red were my sunsets, how clear my dawns!
And flowers smiled along my path
As I passed.

Rachel

In You, O Lord, I take refuge;
   let me never be put to shame.
In Your righteousness deliver me and rescue me;
   incline Your ear to me and save me.
Be to me a rock of refuge,
   a strong fortress, to save me,
     for You are my rock and my fortress.

For you, O Lord, are my hope,
   my trust, O Lord, from my youth.
Upon You I have leaned from my birth;
   it was You who took me from my mother's womb.
My praise is continually of you.

I have been like a portent to many,
    but You are my strong refuge.
My mouth is filled with Your praise,
    and with Your glory all day long.
Do not cast me off in the time of old age;
Do not forsake me when my strength is spent.
For my enemies speak concerning me,
    and those who watch for my life consult together.
They say, "Pursue and seize that person
    whom God has forsaken,
    for there is no one to deliver."

O God, do not be far from me;
    O my God, make haste to help me!
Let my accusers be put to shame and consumed;
    let those who seek to hurt me
    be covered with scorn and disgrace.
But I will hope continually,
    and will praise You yet more and more.
My mouth will tell of Your righteous acts,
    of Your deeds of salvation all day long,
    though their number is past my knowledge.
I will come praising the mighty deeds of the Lord God,
    I will praise Your righteousness, Yours alone.

O God, from my youth you have taught me
    and I still proclaim Your wondrous deeds.
So even to old age and grey hairs,
    O God, do not forsake me,
until I proclaim Your might
    to all the generations to come.
Your power and your righteousness, O God,
    reach the high heavens.

from Psalm 71

14

The Years Pass By

Soon another year will end and a new year will be upon us; for some the passage of time can be depressing. For others, the prospect of a new year brings fresh hope, ideas, and the chance of a new beginning.

For everything there is a season,
    and a time for every purpose under heaven:
A time to be born,
    and a time to die;
A time to plant,
    and a time to pluck up what is planted;
A time to kill,
    and a time to heal;
A time to break down,
    and a time to build up;
A time to weep,
    and a time to laugh;
A time to mourn,
    and a time to dance;
A time to cast away stones,
    and a time to gather stones together;
A time to embrace,
    and a time to refrain from embracing;
A time to seek,

and a time to lose;
A time to keep,
  and a time to discard;
A time to rend,
  and a time to sew;
A time to keep silence,
  and a time to speak;
A time to love,
  and a time to hate;
A time for war,
  and a time for peace.

Ecclesiastes 3.1–8

A man doesn't have time
to have time for everything.
He doesn't have seasons enough to have
a season for every purpose. Ecclesiastes
  was wrong about that.

A man needs to love and to hate
  at the same moment,
to laugh and cry
  with the same eyes,
with the same hands to cast away stones
and to gather them,
to make love in war
  and war in love.

And to hate and forgive
  and remember and forget,
to set in order and confuse,
  to eat and to digest
what history
takes years and years to do.

A man doesn't have time.
When he loses he seeks,
when he finds he forgets,
when he forgets he loves, when he loves
he begins to forget.

And his soul is experienced, his soul
is very professional.
Only his body remains forever
an amateur. It tries and it misses,
gets muddled, doesn't learn a thing,
drunk and blind in its pleasures
and in its pains.

He will die as figs die in autumn,
shrivelled and full of himself and sweet,
the leaves growing dry on the ground,
the bare branches already pointing to the place
where there is time for everything.

Yehuda Amichai

A Commentary on Kohelet
For everything there is a season, and a time for every matter
under the heavens.

A time to be born, and a time to die.
We cannot choose our time of birth, but we can choose our
manner of life. We cannot escape from death, but we can
choose to accept it with courage.

A time to kill, and a time to heal.
Now is the time to begin to remake ourselves, so that we kill
only the ignorance and evil within us and around us; this
work of healing is the teaching of this season of prayer and
repentance.

A time to break down, and a time to build up.
The time has come to break down old habits of thought, in which men are despised who differ from other men. Time now to build up the human image, to be generous in dealing with our fellow men and women.

A time to mourn, and a time to dance.
We mourn with all who suffer loss, and ease their burden with our care; and then we dance and draw them into our circle of joy; that human circle which remains unbroken when God is in our song.

A time to seek, and a time to lose.
Let us seek one another, and find ourselves; let us lose those things within us which cause us to be lost to the true goodness which God has placed within us.

A time to keep silence, and a time to speak.
To keep silence, when to speak would be to hurt our neighbour and bring us shame; to speak out, when silence would be betrayal, when truth must be loud, when the weak need strength, and victims of injustice a champion.

A time to love, and a time to hate.
What shall we love, if not the good, the eternal and the lovely in people and nature? Whom shall we love, if not the ones closest to us? But what shall we hate except hate itself, and all that sets itself with malice against the human race.

A time for God, and a time for man.
We turn to both in loyal love, and pledge ourselves to honour our heritage, to keep our covenant, to live our faith: walking with God, aspiring to perfection, labouring for a better life in a happy world, in a time of peace.

Chaim Stern

The righteous shall flourish like the palm,
   grow tall like the cedar of Lebanon.
Planted in the house of the Eternal One,
   they shall flourish in the courts of our God;
They shall still bear fruit in old age,
   they shall ever be fresh and green,
Proclaiming that God is just,
   my Rock, in whom there is no flaw

Psalm 92.13–16

We learn, slowly, but undeniably, that nothing belongs to us, completely, finally. The job is ended, the children grow up and move away, even the money (when there is money) buys little that we want. For what we want cannot be bought. And it is then, if ever, that we learn to make our peace with destiny; to accept the fact that our dreams have been half-realised; or unrealised; that we did not do what we set out to do; that our goals have receded as we approached them. There may be a sadness in this prospect, but also a serenity. Illusions lose their power to disturb us; we value life by what it has given us, not by the promise of tomorrow. For only by accepting Time can we, in a measure, learn to conquer it.

Sidney J. Harris

Remember now thy Creator in the days of thy youth, while the evil days come not, nor the years draw nigh, when thou shalt say, I have no pleasure in them;
While the sun, or the light, or the moon, or the stars, be not darkened, nor the clouds return after the rain:
In the day when the keepers of the house shall tremble, and the strong men shall bow themselves, and the grinders cease

because they are few, and those that look out of the windows
be darkened,
And the doors shall be shut in the streets, when the sound of
the grinding is low, and he shall rise up at the voice of the
bird, and all the daughters of musick shall be brought low;
Also when they shall be afraid of that which is high, and
fears shall be in the way, and the almond tree shall flourish,
and the grasshopper shall be a burden, and desire shall fail:
because man goeth to his long home, and the mourners go
about the streets:
Or ever the silver cord be loosed, or the golden bowl be
broken, or the pitcher be broken at the fountain, or the
wheel broken at the cistern.
Then shall the dust return to the earth as it was: and the
spirit shall return unto God who gave it.

Ecclesiastes 12.1–7

A Prayer of the Rabbis

May you live to see your world fulfilled
May your destiny be
    for worlds still to come;
and may you trust in generations past
    and yet to be.

May your heart be filled with intuition
    And your words be filled with insight.
May songs of praise ever be upon your tongue
and your vision be on a straight path before you.
May your eyes shine
    with the light of holy words
and your face reflect
    the brightness of the heavens.

HIGH AND HOLY DAYS

May your lips ever speak wisdom
and your fulfilment be in righteousness
even as you ever yearn to hear the words
of the Holy Ancient One of Old.

Lawrence Kushner

15

Full Moon of Elul

Only half a month remains until the old year ends; the full light of the moon can lighten our inner darkness and give us fresh energy as we move inexorably towards a new year.

From the beginning of Elul onwards, whenever we write a personal letter, we should mention at the beginning that we are praying on our friend's behalf for a good year to come. For instance, "May you be inscribed and sealed for a good year", or "May He who suspends the earth over nothingness, inscribe you for life on this day of good will."

Maharil

A Prayer
For A. A. Wolmark
Oh, God, in painting on the canvas of my life,
Use colours that are strong and rich:
And do not scrape them with the palette-knife,
To make them smooth and thin. I care not which
You use of all Your colours, red or gold,
Purple or black, so that they stand out bold,
And are not lost in muddy, greyish tone;
Heap them on thickly, in a pattern strange, my own;
So that my life be strong and true.

Fill it with joy, or else with sorrows pack;
Paint as You will, but this thing do:
Use colour, even if it be Your deepest black.

Joseph Leftwich

Each of us possesses a Holy Spark, but not everyone exhibits it to the best advantage. It is like the diamond which cannot cast its lustre if buried in the earth. But when disclosed in its appropriate setting there is light, as from a diamond, in each of us.

Israel Friedman of Ruzhin

Love for My People
I know a flower that grows and blooms
Without dew or rain.
It has no need of sun or wind.
It thrives in gloom and pain.

It grows in storms and snow,
When all flowers die.
The storm gives it strength and sap,
Fragrance and brilliancy.
When thunder and lightning crash,
And great trees fall,
It lifts its head, refreshed and bright,
Radiant over all.

The flower is love of my people.
It blossoms in the storm.
It draws its sap from suffering,
And the cold blast keeps it warm.

Yehoash

Without telling his teacher anything of what he was doing, a disciple of Rabbi Baruch's had inquired into the nature of God, and in his thinking had penetrated further and further until he was tangled in doubts, and what had been certain up to this time became uncertain.

When Rabbi Baruch noticed that the young man no longer came to him as usual, he went to the city where he lived, entered his room unexpectedly, and said to him: "I know what is hidden in your heart. You have passed through the fifty gates of reason. You begin with a question and think, and think up an answer – and the first gate opens to a new question! And again you plumb it, find the solution, fling open the second gate – and look into a new question. And on and on like this, deeper and deeper, until you have forced open the fiftieth gate. There you stare at the question whose answer no man has ever found, for if there were one who knew it, there would no longer be freedom of choice. But if you dare to probe still further, you plunge into the abyss."

"So should I go back all the way, to the very beginning?" cried the disciple.

"If you turn you will not be going back," said Rabbi Baruch. "You will be standing beyond the last gate: You will stand in faith."

Martin Buber

Draw from the past, live in the present, work for the future.

Abraham Geiger

It is appropriate to study spiritually uplifting books in order to awaken our hearts to Teshuvah, and to engage less in other studies during the Penitential days. To the same effect wrote Rabbi Hayyim Joseph David Azulai [Birke Yosef; 18th cent.]: "I have seen that some of the rabbis, who are always engaged in the study of the Law, set aside part of their regular curriculum during the month of Elul to recite penitential prayers and supplications."

S. Y. Agnon

16

Study

Study is at the centre of Jewish life: it is even said that "the ignorant cannot be pious". Only after a sincere intellectual effort to understand the meaning of prayer, repentance and divine forgiveness will we be truly ready for the key task of the High Holy Days.

These are actions which bring
benefit here and now but whose
full value can be measured only
in the light of eternity:
honouring one's father and mother;
acts of love and kindness;
diligent pursuit of knowledge and wisdom;
hospitality to strangers;
visiting the sick;
enabling bride and groom to rejoice;
consoling the bereaved;
praying with sincerity;
and making peace where there is strife.
And the study of Torah leads to them all.

Mishnah

Talk of rewards we are to receive both in this world and the next does not seem high-minded enough for some of our teachers. If Torah is so wondrous a gift, then we should pursue it simply to fill our lives with its words and sacred meaning: "Do not say, 'I will read the Bible that I may be called a sage; I will investigate the traditions that I may be called a rabbi; I will study that I may be called an elder and sit in the assembly of elders'; but study out of love and let what honours come as may . . ." R. Eliezer b. R. Zadok said: "Do good deeds because of your regard for their Commander and study the words of Torah for their own sake. Do not use them as a crown to magnify yourself with, or as a spade to hoe with" (Ned.62a). Though this idea is a noble one, it clashes with dominant motifs of western civilisation. Too often we are taught to become paragons of pragmatism or even opportunism, calculating our profit before investing much effort. Even if the understanding of "what's in it for me" is subtle and refined, like elevating our humanity or making us better people, we too often live with our eyes on the prize instead of the task before us. Of course, all of our sages believed there are great rewards in studying and living by the Torah. But those who preached the vision of *Torah lishmah* did so from their passionate conviction of the intrinsic worth of studying God's word.

Eugene B. Borowitz & Frances Weinman Schwartz

תַּלְמוּד תּוֹרָה, *Talmud Torah*, means both to learn and to teach the literature in which our people have recorded, and continue to record, their understanding of God's will. It is, in short, the whole task of Jewish religious education. As such, it stands supreme among our obligations. For everything depends on it: the spiritual well-being of every individual and of every generation, the transmission of our heritage and its distinctive contribution to civilisation.

John D. Rayner

"You can learn something from everything", the Rabbi of Sadagora once said to his Hasidim. "Everything can teach us something, and not only everything God has created. What man has made can also teach us something."

"What can we learn from a train?" one Hasid asked dubiously.

"That, because of one second, one can miss everything."

"And from the telegraph?"

"That every word is counted and charged."

"And the telephone?"

"That what we say here is heard there."

Martin Buber

The Hafetz Hayyim said: "Do not say 'and teach them (the words) to your children,' but say rather: 'and study the words yourselves.' No one can be certain that his children will maintain their father's eagerness to study and learn subjects of Torah."

Louis I. Newman

Rabban Gamliel, the son of Rabbi Judah the Prince, said: An excellent thing is the study of the Torah combined with some worldly occupation, for the labour demanded by them both makes sin to be forgotten. All study of the Torah without work must in the end be futile, and become the cause of sin.

Mishnah

Those who study the Torah in order to learn and do God's will acquire many merits: and not only that, but the whole world is indebted to them. They are cherished as friends of God and of their fellow human beings. It clothes them with humility and reverence; it enables them to become righteous and saintly, upright and faithful; it keeps them far from sin, and brings them near to virtue; they benefit mankind with counsel and knowledge, wisdom and strength. They become like a never-failing fountain, and like a river that grows ever mightier as it flows. They are modest, slow to anger and forgiving of insults; and it magnifies and exalts them above all things.

Mishnah

17

Tikkun Olam

This is the essential religious task of our time: to bring some improvement to this needful world through acts of reconciliation, conservation, charity, and loving kindness.

A single person was created in the world in order to teach that if one had caused a single soul to perish, it is as if one had thereby destroyed an entire world; and if one saved a single life, it is as if one had thereby saved an entire world.

Mishnah

Trusting in you, Eternal God, we hope soon to behold the glory of Your might, when false gods will vanish from our hearts and idolatry cease forever. Help us to perfect the world by bringing it under Your unchallenged rule, when all will invoke Your name, relinquish evil, and turn to You alone.

Siddur Lev Chadash

Each lifetime is the pieces of a jigsaw puzzle.
For some there are more pieces,
For others the puzzle is more difficult to assemble.

Some seem to be born with a nearly completed puzzle.
And so it goes.
Souls trying this way and that
Trying to assemble the myriad parts.

But know this. No one has within themselves
All the pieces to his or her puzzle.
Like before the days they used to seal
jigsaw puzzles in cellophane. Insuring that
all the pieces were there.

Everyone carries with them at least one and probably
Many pieces to someone else's puzzle.

Sometimes they know it.
Sometimes they don't.

And when you present your piece
Which is worthless to you,
to another, whether you know it or not,
Whether they know it or not,
You are a messenger from the Most High.

Lawrence Kushner

To open eyes when others close them
to hear when others do not wish to listen
to look when others turn away
to seek to understand when others give up
to rouse oneself when others accept
to continue the struggle even when one is not the strongest
to cry out when others keep silent –
to be a Jew
is that,
it is first of all that

and further
to live when others are dead
and to remember when others have forgotten.

Emmanuel Eydoux

I believe that God is the source of holiness and sanctity in the Universe. I believe that men and women and children can draw constantly closer to that Source when we exercise our capacities to say no to, and to translate our no, to destruction, hatred, egotism, prejudice, untrammelled possessiveness, uncontrolled megalomania. The sacred is that dimension of being which propels us into the search for love, awe, and reverence . . . which allows us to create for the morrow a world that is better than yesterday . . . the power of decision to ensure, as much as we are able, that there will be a morrow.

Marshall T. Meyer

. . . The Jewish passion for social justice had made a difference not only to Jews but to all the world. The refusal to yield to despair, fatigue, or cynicism; the stubborn belief in *tikkun olam* (repairing the world); the *chutzpadik* notion that we are partners with God in refashioning a humane and civilised world – these Jewish compulsions have helped preserve the Jewish spirit.

Albert Vorspan

A *Techine* for Yom Kippur

O God, Creator of Heaven and Earth, Creator of humankind and of all living things, grant me the power to feel as others feel, the power to listen and to hear, to behold and truly see, to touch and be touched.

Keep fresh within me the memory of my own suffering and the suffering of *clal yisrael* (the whole community), not in order to stimulate eternal paranoia, but rather that I may better understand the suffering of strangers; and may that understanding lead me to do everything in my power to alleviate and to prevent such suffering.

When I see streams of refugees bearing the pathetic belongings they have salvaged from ruined homes, may I recall the wanderings of the people of Israel and may I vow never to be the cause of loss and homelessness.

Enable me to be like Yourself – to feed the hungry, clothe the naked, tend the sick, comfort the bereaved. Guide me in the ways of *tikkun olam*, of mending the world.

Grant me the wisdom to know what is right and what is wrong and inspire me with the courage to speak out whenever I see injustice, without shame or fear of personal retribution. Enable me to feel pity even for my enemies. Grant me the will and the ability to be a peacemaker, so that the day may soon come when all people will live in friendship and Your tabernacle of peace will spread over all the dwellers on earth. Amen.

Alice Shalvi

18

Personal Responsibility

No one else is to blame for the mistakes we make, the angry words and thoughtless deeds. At this season we must face up to our failings and resolve to improve every facet of our lives.

Once on Rosh Hashanah about the time for afternoon prayers, Rabbi Mendel entered the synagogue and found about forty of his Hasidim there who had come from a long distance to spend the holy day with him.

"This is a splendid congregation," he said. "But know all of you that I cannot carry all of you on my shoulders. Each one of you must work for himself."

Martin Buber

There are many fine things which you mean to do some day, in what you think will be more favourable circumstances. But the only time that is surely yours is the present; hence this is the time to speak the word of appreciation and sympathy, to do the generous deed, to forgive the fault of a thoughtless friend, to sacrifice self a little more for others. Today is the day in which to express your noblest qualities of heart and mind, to do at least one worthy thing which you have long postponed, and to use your God-given abilities

for the enrichment of some less fortunate fellow traveller.
Today you can make your life significant and worthwhile.
The present is yours to do with as you will.

Grenville Kleiser

God give us the strength
    to transcend setbacks and pain
    to put our difficulties into perspective

God give us the strength
    to fight against all forms of injustice,
    whether they be subtle or easily apparent

God give us the strength
    to take the path less travelled
    and more disturbing

God give us the strength
    to persevere
    to reach out to those in need –
    may we abandon none of your creations

May we never become callous or apathetic because
    of our own disappointments

May our personal pain never be used as
    an excuse to stop heeding your call

God give us the strength
    to continually strive to do more

Let us always strive to give, even if we,
    ourselves, feel alone or impoverished

For we must always strive to reach beyond
    ourselves.

Angela Graboys & Laura Rappaport

It is not enough for me to be able to say: "I am". I want to know *who I am*, and in relation to whom I live. It is not enough for me to ask questions; I want to know how to answer the one question that seems to encompass everything I face: What am I here for?

What is the meaning of my being? My quest is not for theoretical knowledge about myself. What I look for is not how to gain a firm hold on myself and on life, but primarily how to live a life that would deserve and evoke an eternal Amen.

Anon

Rabbi Bunam said to his Hasidim:
"The sins which man commits – those are not his great crime. Temptation is powerful and his strength is slight! The great crime of man is that he can turn at every moment, and does not do so."

Martin Buber

Peace is not the absence of conflict.
Peace is dealing with conflict
while honouring justice.
Peace is not the absence of anger.
Peace is expressing anger
while honouring compassion.
Peace is not the absence of desire.
Peace is allowing for desire without
the fantasy that fulfilment brings happiness.
Peace is not the absence of fear.
Peace is knowing how to move through fear.
Peace is not the absence of self.
Peace is knowing that the self is absent.

May I cultivate the skills to live in peace:
to live with honour,
to live with justice,
to live with compassion,
to live with desire,
to live with fear,
to live with self,
to live with emptiness.

Rami Shapiro

How do we find our Creator
who is in heaven?
We find God by good deeds
and study of Torah.
And the Holy One, ever to
be praised, finds us
through love, through
community, through respect,
through companionship,
through truth, through peace,
through a good heart,
through decency,
through No that is really No,
through Yes that is really Yes.

Midrash

19

Self-Examination

We cannot easily hide the truth from ourselves, though we may try to avoid it. The High Holy Days confront us with who and what we really are and inspire us to change.

Today we stand before the Mirror of All
to see ourselves as we are.
We come with no gifts, no bribes, no illusions, no more
  excuses.
We stand without defence and wait to be filled.
What will fill us?
Remorse, certainly. So much error and needless pain.
And joy: remembered moments of love and right doing.
We are too complex for single-sided emotions.
And we are too simple to be excused by our complexity.
Let us be bold enough to see,
humble enough to feel,
daring enough to turn and
embrace the way of justice, mercy and simplicity.

Rami Shapiro

The Rabbi of Berditchev saw a man hurrying along the street, looking neither right nor left. "Why are you rushing so?" he asked the man.

"I am after my livelihood," the man replied.

"And how do you know," continued the rabbi, "that your livelihood is running on before you, so that you have to rush after it? Perhaps it is behind you, and all you need do to encounter it is to stand still – but you are running away from it!"

Martin Buber

Ben Zoma used to say:

Who is wise? One who learns from every person, as it says, "From all my teachers I have gained understanding."

Who is mighty? One who exercises self-control, as it says, "One slow to anger is better than a hero, and one who practises self-restraint than one who conquers a city."

Who is rich? One who is content with life's portion, as it says, "When you eat what you have worked for, you will be happy, and it will be well with you."

Who is respected? One who respects others, as it says, "For those who respect Me I will respect, and those who despise Me will be held in contempt."

Mishnah

In Greek, the word for prayer means "to wish for", in German it means "to beg", and in English "to entreat" or "implore". However, the Hebrew word *tefillah*, prayer, is derived from a verb meaning "to judge". The act of praying is expressed by the reflexive form of the verb meaning "to judge oneself". In Judaism, the act of prayer implies self-examination as an essential preliminary to communication with God.

Editors

Rabba taught:
When, after his death, a man is led before the judgement seat
of God, he will be asked the following questions:
Did you conduct your business affairs with integrity?
Did you set aside fixed times for the study of the Torah?
Did you fulfil the commandment of procreation?
Did you hope for salvation?
Did you occupy yourself dialectically with wisdom?
Did you learn to understand how one thing follows from
another?

Talmud

Man is the only creature endowed with conscience. His
conscience is the voice which calls him back to himself; it
permits him to know what he ought to do in order to become
himself; it helps him to remain aware of the aims of his life
and of the norms necessary for the attainment of these aims.
We are therefore not helpless victims of circumstance; we
are, indeed, able to change and to influence forces inside and
outside ourselves and to control, at least to some extent, the
conditions which play upon us.

Erich Fromm

Our Father, when I am overcome by a sense of weakness,
so that I feel unequal to the tasks before me, or
oppressed by the burdens of life, or daunted by difficulties,
Give me strength.

When my heart is cast down by sorrow, or anxiety
takes hold of me; when I am pained by suffering, whether in
my life or in the life of others,
Give me courage and hope.

But when I feel the happiness of life, rejoicing in all that
enriches, in the fulfilment of my desires, or in some event
which brings special gladness to my heart,
Give me the sense of dependence upon thee, my God,
so that I lay before thee the offering of my grateful joy.

Liberal Jewish Prayer Book

20

Good and Bad Inclination

The rabbis taught that we are given free will so that we may choose the path we shall follow; will our thoughts and deeds incline towards the good or the bad?

When God created man He created him with two impulses, the *yetzer ha-tov* and the *yetzer ha-ra*, both the good and evil inclination.

Talmud

When God had created man He found His work *tov me-od*, very good. Now t*ov* stands for the inclination toward good and *me-od* for the opposite. But can the evil impulse be at all considered good? Yes, for were it not for this impulse no man would build a house, take a wife, or beget children.

Midrash

A villager lamented to the Kobriner that his evil desires constantly overcame him and caused him to fall into transgression.

"Do you ride a horse?" the rabbi inquired.
"Yes", answered the villager.
"What do you do if you happen to fall off?"

"I mount again," said the villager.

"Well, imagine the Evil Impulse to be the horse," remarked the rabbi. "If you fall, mount again. Eventually you will master it."

Louis I. Newman

The evil inclination grows stronger against us from day to day, and seeks to destroy us; and if the Holy One, ever to be praised, did not help us, we would not be able to prevail over it.

Talmud

When we do something which shows some moral weakness, the act is frequently condoned by the comment: It is human. The use of "human" in such contexts has given it a connotation of weakness. It is human to err, it is human to satisfy the desires of the flesh even when it can be done only by ignoring the best moral standards, it is human to obey instincts which inhere in our humanity, it is human to yield to temptations. But there is another side to our nature. It is not only human to be weak but it is also human to have "a touch of the Divine". It is not only human to feel temptation but it is also human to resist. Every day men and women make sacrifices to help others. By the power of the spirit they overcome the force of mere instincts. Their victory is the triumph of the human over the human. It is human to be weak. It is also human to be strong.

Israel I. Mattuck

With the Rabbis we may speak of the Yetzer as a neutral endowment, which we ourselves turn into good or into evil. Our instinctual responses and cravings become evil when they are permitted to run wild and to grow into lusts for pleasure, for glory or for power in disregard of reason and of social well-being. No inherited and ineradicable taint keeps the soul from virtue. Man never was vitiated to the point of losing divine likeness or his ability to partake of God's grace. Sin springs from the mind and the will of man, from his weakness and ignorance.

John D. Rayner

Our God and God of all generations, help us to overcome the impulse to do evil. You have created us able to do Your will, but in our nature there is a wayward spirit that hinders us and keeps us from doing what we should. Eternal God help us to subdue it, so that we may, with a whole heart, make Your will our own.

Talmud

21

Humility

Genuine humility is defined by a sense of our smallness in the universe; an added awareness of the greatness of God may also inspire us to avoid sin.

To begin with oneself, but not to end with oneself;
to start with oneself, but not to aim at oneself;
to comprehend oneself, but not to be preoccupied with
   oneself.

Martin Buber

Hineni
here I am again
without much to offer by way of moral worth
I've a rich collection of defeats
maybe that's to your liking?
I don't know, do you?
if I'm to be quite frank
your likes and dislikes have never been
all that clear to me
presumably love is something you're in favour of
and I've found it possible to love
but never without a certain anguish
whether that's the way you intended it
or that's a problem all my own

I can't say, can you?
I've never wanted to pain myself
I guess I can plead good intentions
but I needn't tell you about good intentions
and the road to hell
I've often wondered: did you yourself intend
when you got it all going
that to live would be so complicated
to find a way in the world so hazardous?
did you have any idea at all
that living would involve such confusion
and such heartbreak?
I can't be sure any of this will mean much to you
I can't even be sure that you exist
as more than a figment of my own mysterious psyche
it's a risk to open up to you
who knows, I may be branding myself a terrible fool
but what's not a risk? what's guaranteed to be foolproof?
so here I am again
praying for some modest bravery
so that I can go on saying to you: here
I am again.

Stanley F. Chyet

It was a favourite saying of the Rabbis of Javneh: I am a
creature of God and my neighbour is also His creature; my
work is in the city and his is in the field; I rise early to
my work, and he rises early to his. As he cannot excel in my
work, so I cannot excel in his work. But perhaps you say, I
do great things, and he does small things. We have learnt
that it matters not whether a man does much or little, if only
he direct his heart to heaven.

Talmud

Guard me
from vicious leanings and haughty ways,
from anger and from temper,
from melancholy, talebearing,
and from all the other evil qualities.

Nor let envy of any man rise in my heart,
nor envy of me in the heart of others.

On the contrary:
put it in my heart that I may see my comrades' virtue
and not their failing.

Elimelech of Lizhensk

Te Deum
Not because of victories
I sing,
having none,
but for the common sunshine,
the breeze,
the largesse of the spring.

Not for victory
but for the day's work done
as well as I was able;
not for a seat upon the dais
but at the common table.

Charles Reznikoff

Before I was born, I had no significance. And now that I have
been born, I am of equal worth. Dust am I though I live;
surely after death will I be dust. In Your Presence, aware of
my frailty, I am totally embarrassed and confused. May it be
Your will, Lord my God and God of my fathers, to help me

abstain from further sin. With Your great compassion wipe away the sins I have committed against You, though not by means of suffering.

Keep me far from petty thoughts and petty pride, far from anger, impatience, despair, gossip and all bad traits.

Let me not be overwhelmed by jealousy of others; let others not be overwhelmed by jealousy of me. Grant me the gift of seeing other people's merits, not their faults.

He who brings peace to His universe will bring peace to us and to all the people Israel. And let us say: Amen.

Elimelech of Lizhensk

God on high, divine
   Sovereign,
Enlighten my soul at all
   times.
Give me, O God, true faith;
and perfect humility
against the world's vanities.
Do not give me riches, O
   God,
that may make me proud;
nor poverty,
that may abase me.
Give me, O God, some help
that I may serve You,
and life that I may praise
   You.

Alto Senhor, Rei divino,
alumiai a minha alma de
   continuo.
Dai-me, Senhor, fé direita,
e humildade perfeita,
contra as vaidades do
   mundo.
Não me deis, Senhor,
   riqueza,
com que me ensoberbe,
nem pobreza,
que me abata.
Dai-me, Senhor, remédio
com que vos sirva,
vida com que vos louve.

Marrano Prayer

22

Human Nature

What makes us who and what we are? We share so much with other human beings, yet each one of us has our own personality and abilities. Our challenge is to make the best of who we are and what we are. We alone can choose to do so.

Is there a person anywhere altogether righteous, who never sins? I am but flesh and blood, often yielding to temptation: I am human, often torn by conflicts.

Man is not an angel, nor a robot. God's gift to us is the power and the freedom to choose. We are forever faced with choices of good and evil, blessings and curses. The struggle is ceaseless: the choice is ours.

Abraham Danzig

Guard me, Oh God,
   from hating man my brother,
Guard me from recalling what,
   from my early youth, to me he did.
When all the stars in my sky are quenched,
   within me my soul's voice grows mute –
When I am overcome by disaster,
   let me not lay bare his guilt.

For he is my hidden dwelling-place,
   in him am I reflected again,
Like a wayfarer from the planets,
   beholding his face in a pool.
What use is all my struggle,
   to whom shall I wail out the pain
If hollow, blemished
   is my distant night's moon?

When the gates are locked,
   darkness over the city reclining,
And emptied of love, rejected,
   I am bound to my rock:
Permit me to see in him a spark,
   only a spark still shining,
That I may know that in myself,
   in me, all is not yet snuffed out.

Shin Shalom

Rabbi Yochanan ben Zakkai said to his disciples:
What is a right path?
Rabbi Eliezer said: A good eye.
Rabbi Joshua said: A good friend.
Rabbi Yosé said: A good neighbour.
Rabbi Simeon said: Foresight.
Rabbi Elazar said: A good heart.
He said to them:
I prefer the words of Elazar ben Arach, for his words include
all of yours.

Mishnah

HIGH AND HOLY DAYS

A man is known by three names. The first is the name which his parents give him; the second is the name by which others call him; and the third is the name by which he is identified in the true record of his life, from birth to death.

Midrash

Each of us has a name given us by God and by our father and mother.

Each of us has a name given us by our stature and smile and the clothes we wear.

Each of us has a name given us by the mountains and the walls within which we live.

Each of us has a name given us by the planets and by our neighbours.

Each of us has a name given us by our sins and by our aspirations.

Each of us has a name given us by our enemies and by those we love.

Each of us has a name given us by our leisure time and by our work.

Each of us has a name given us by the seasons and by our blindness.

Each of us has a name given us by the sea and by the way we die.

Zelda Mishkofsky

With regard to all human traits, the middle of the road is the right path. For example: Do not be hot-tempered, easily angered. Nor, on the other hand, should you be unfeeling like a corpse. Rather, take the middle of the road: keep an even disposition, reserving your anger for occasions when it is truly warranted. Similarly, do not cultivate a desire for luxuries; keep your eye fixed only on genuine necessities. In giving to others, do not hold back what you can afford, but do not give so lavishly that you yourself will be impoverished. Avoid both hysterical gaiety and sombre dejection, and instead be calmly joyful always, showing a cheerful countenance. Act similarly with regard to all the dispositions. This is the path followed by the wise.

Moses Maimonides

Alone among God's creatures, it would seem, we have been given freedom to choose between good and evil. That freedom is both our glory and our burden. For our choices have consequences. Sublime achievements, horrendous crimes: both lie within our grasp. And because our nature is twofold – noble and creative on the one hand, selfish and destructive on the other – the future is open.

John D. Rayner

23

Selichot

Prayer is possible at any time, but there is something about the midnight hour or the breaking of dawn that seem to make it easier to reveal our weakness to a loving and forgiving God.

It is customary to rise towards dawn and to say prayers of forgiveness and supplication from the beginning of Elul onwards. The custom of the Ashkenazi communities is not so, but rather from the beginning of Elul the shofar is blown every day after the morning service . . . and they rise towards dawn to recite Selichot from the Sunday preceding Rosh Hashanah, and if Rosh Hashanah falls on a Monday or a Tuesday, then they start from the Sunday before that.

Shulchan Aruch

We have come to seek Your presence, for our awareness of love and truth comes from You.

God, do not increase our shame! Do not send us away empty from this service. Forgive us! Let salvation and mercy come to us from every place where You dwell.

We have come, asking You for inner peace. Tremendous and awesome though You are, You are our security whenever we are troubled.

Let the grace of new life come to us as we pray! Pardon us!
Send us forgiveness and mercy from every place where You
dwell.

Machzor

The happenings of this world take place
not in the sphere between two principles,
light and darkness, good and evil,
but in the sphere between God and men,
these mortal, brittle human beings
who are able to face God and withstand His word.

Adam's sin did not happen once and for all,
it did not become an inevitable fate for everyone,
but it continually happens here and now in all its reality.
In spite of all past history,
in spite of all that has come before,
each of us stands in the naked condition of Adam:
each of us must make the decision.

Martin Buber

Selichot
In darkening shade
lies city street,
in deepening shadow
wood and meadow,
and barren and shallow
our thoughts tonight.

    Through blackened window
    through tight closed door
    no wind can wander,

no light can enter,
empty our hearts
and fallow and blight.

Now do we ask of You
deep in Your universe,
far in Your wanderings,
Maker so merciful,
Open Your cloudbanks
to moon full and bright.

Let moonlight
illumine us,
night winds
come brushing us,
breath of Your presence
be felt in our souls.

Ruth F. Brin

A man must learn to be strong that he will be able to yield
when necessary.

Israel Salanter

The Penitential Season is a challenge to us to free our soul
by turning it towards God. God has given us a standard of
life, and when we fall below that standard, we weaken our
personality and deface the image of God in which we were
created. "Against Thee only have I sinned, and done that
which is evil in Thy sight." So says the Psalmist. Man's self-
esteem is degraded. He cries out for forgiveness to his God.

Lily H. Montagu

Merciful God, we have come to call upon You; have mercy upon us.

Merciful God, cover us with Your glory.

Merciful God, do not chastise us according to our wrongdoings.

Merciful God, pardon and forgive our sins and iniquities.

Merciful God, open the heavens to our prayers.

Merciful God, grant us a good year.

Merciful God, confirm us in the Book of Life.

Sephardi Machzor

24

The Will to Change

God does not predetermine whether we will be righteous or wicked, that is left to each one of us to decide for ourselves. We have the capacity to decide, but we need the will to decide correctly.

For two-and-a-half years the Schools of Shammai and Hillel remained divided. The former said: It would have been better if humankind had never been created. The latter said: It is better that humankind was created. After the debate, they reached a consensus: It would have been better had humankind not been created; now that we are here, however, let us look to our conduct.

Talmud

Everyone has been given free will. If we wish to turn to the good way and be righteous, we have the power to do so; and if we wish to turn to the evil way and be wicked, we are free to do that. Everyone is capable of being righteous like Moses or wicked like Jeroboam, learned or ignorant, merciful or cruel, mean or generous. Nobody forces us, or decides for us, pulls us in one direction or the other; but we, by our own volition, choose the path we wish to follow.

Moses Maimonides

Seek the Eternal, your God, whom you shall find, if you seek with all your heart and soul (Deuteronomy 4.29).

We can choose the way of our life. Not in all things of life have we a choice: fortune, fate or circumstance have a hand in the succession of events that make up my life; and even in what I am, environment or heredity, or both, have had a share, limiting my capacities and powers, and so putting bounds to the possibilities of achievement. But life presents to every person the power to choose how one shall live.

Liberal Jewish Prayer Book

Each evening before he went to sleep it was the custom of Rabbi Levi Yitzchak to take a *Cheshbon ha-Nefesh* – that is, to examine his thoughts and deeds for that day. If he found a blemish in them, he would say to himself, "Levi Yitzchak will not do that again."

Then he would chide himself, "Levi Yitzchak, you said the same thing yesterday."

Then he would reply, "Yesterday Levi Yitzchak did not speak the truth. Today he speaks the truth."

There is no final conquest of self. The ego is too elusive, subtle, and deceiving. It is an eternal struggle demanding eternal vigilance.

Samuel H. Dresner

We are told by the Psalmist first to leave evil and then to do good. I will add that if you find it difficult to follow this advice, you may first do good, and the evil will automatically depart from you.

Yitzchak Meir of Ger

Of the Chasidic Saint, Levi Yitzchak of Berditchev, it is related that once, during the solemn period between New Year and the Day of Atonement, he stood at the door of his house, dull, lifeless, altogether out of tune with the season, lethargic under all calls to penitence. And as he stood so, a cobbler came by, looking for work. Spying the Rabbi he called: "Have you nothing that needs mending?"

"Have I nothing that needs mending?" Levi Yitzchak echoed reflectively. Then his heart contracted within him and he wept. He wept for his sins, for all those things in his soul and life that needed mending . . . Only, why, instead of weeping, did he not do with his soul as he would with his shoes? . . .

Martin Buber

You know the thoughts of men and women,
And read the minds of mortals.
You know that with all my heart I wish to serve You.
That each and every day I ask that my way leads me to
    deserve Your laws.

But you know that I am tangled in the web of baser
    instincts by which you test me, and surrounded by the
    temptations of the world by which You try me,
Until my heart is in turmoil and my strength fails me.
So that they prevent me from thinking of You with a clean
    hand and a pure heart,
From pursuing what is right and just, and doing what is
    right and true.

Therefore I will pour out before You prayers and
    meditations to arouse my dormant spirit from its sleep.

THE WILL TO CHANGE

Full well I know that You are not appeased by endless words
    nor reached by murmuring lips,
But only by contrition, humility and tenderness of heart.

Bachya ibn Pakuda

25

Wisdom

The continuing search for wisdom is the hallmark of men and women who are truly wise; those who possess wisdom are a blessing to those around them and a source of strength in times of trouble and anxiety.

Happy are those who find wisdom,
and those who get understanding.
For her income is better than silver,
and her revenue than fine gold.
She is more precious than jewels,
and nothing you desire can compare with her.
Long life is in her right hand;
in her left are riches and honour.
Her ways are ways of pleasantness,
and all her paths are peace.
She is a tree of life to those who lay hold of her;
those who hold her fast are called happy.

Proverbs 3.13–18

The world is new to us
    every morning –
    that is God's gift

and we should believe
   we are reborn each day.

Baal Shem Tov

A fool and a sage both have seven traits:
The wise never speak before the wiser.
They do not interrupt their companion;
they are not afraid to reply;
they ask to the point and reply as they should;
they speak of first things first and of last things last.
If they have not heard they say, I have not heard.
They acknowledge the truth.
The reverse is true of fools.

Mishnah

They prayed metaphysics, acrostics, angelology, Cabala, history, exegesis, talmudical controversies, menus, recipes, priestly prescriptions, the canonical books, psalms, love-poems ... If they did not always know what they were saying, they always meant it.

Israel Zangwill

Above all, my children, be honest in money matters with Jews and non-Jews alike. If you have money or possessions belonging to other people, take better care of them than you would if they were your own. The first question that is put to a person on entering the next world is whether or not one was faithful in one's business dealings.

Glueckel of Hameln

My father used to say, "Show me a person who has no problems and I'll show you a fool." Too many Jews today want to solve everything, find simple solutions and answers – as if all we have are simple questions – when actually we have profound and exciting problems. I like the struggle and the conflicts. I don't want to live in a fool's paradise.

Susannah Heschel

Thus says the Lord, Let not the wise man glory in his wisdom, nor let the mighty man glory in his might, let not the rich man glory in his riches;

But let him who glories glory in this, that he understands and knows me, that I am the Lord who exercises loving kindness, justice, and righteousness, in the earth; for in these things I delight, says the Lord.

Jeremiah 9.22–23

26

Human Suffering

The Book of Job makes clear that suffering need not be a consequence of sin. Human nobility comes from seeking to rise above our suffering and refusing to allow it to embitter our outlook on life.

Ten trials were inflicted upon Abraham,
and he withstood them all.
Why?
To show how great was his commitment.

Suffering is the stuff of life,
and through suffering
one opens the heart to compassion,
the shared pain of living beings.

We withstand our trials
by feeling the pain without abandoning the world.

Suffering without bitterness,
we do justly, even in the face of unjust adversity.

Rami Shapiro

A god once commanded us to stand strong
under the terrible tree of life.
And in the black wind of the years we stood,

stricken with expectation
perhaps the fruit would fall at our feet.
But nothing happened.

And on the day of secret reckoning
Between him and us
we saw a hunched landscape, brown leaves falling,
and felt on our faces
a cold wind blowing.

Then said a Voice: this is your day of freedom.
This is everything. And this is good.

Now towards the flame of cutting cold, alone,
I take
a few steps only
until I meet
that flickering lantern
at the corner of the street.

Leah Goldberg

If we could hang all our sorrows on pegs and were allowed
to choose those we liked best, everyone of us would take
back his own, for all the rest would seem even more difficult
to bear.

Martin Buber

In times of darkness when my heart is grieved,
When despair besieges my mind
And my days are a weariness of living –
Then is my life like the flower that struggles to grow
Where no ray of sun ever penetrates;
Then is my spirit pent up within me
And my soul is shut in like a night of darkness.

When such darkness overtakes me, O God,
Fortify my mind with trust in life.
Let not the blight of futility engulf my existence.
Knit up the sinews of my strength still to struggle.
Drive on the will within me to ceaseless exertion
Until my powers break through my mortal toils
And blaze forth with the strength of Thy Spirit.

Jacob L. Halevi

I think I have lost something along the way,
What it is I do not know.
Shall I turn back? It is so far off now.
Yet it is a pity to let it go.

I have lost something, but do not know what.
Is it anything of worth?
I shall let it lie – for the day is short,
And vast is the earth.

Already the shadows fall from the trees.
Long falls my shadow.
My heart is unquiet. It cries – turn back.
My loss torments me so.

So I stand still in the midst of the road,
Tormented, doubt-tossed.
I have lost something, but do not know what.
But I know that I've lost.

Abraham Reisen

Perish the day on which I was born,
And the night it was announced,
"A male has been conceived!"
May that day be darkness;

May God above have no concern for it;
May light not shine on it;

Why does God give light to the sufferer
And life to the bitter in spirit;
To those who wait for death but it does not come,
Who search for it more than for treasure,
Who rejoice to exultation,
And are glad to reach the grave;
To the man who has lost his way,
Whom God has hedged about?

My groaning serves as my bread;
My roaring pours forth as water.
For what I feared has overtaken me;
What I dreaded has come upon me.
I had no repose, no quiet, no rest,
And trouble came.

Job 3.3–4, 20–26

You have called me into life, setting me in the midst of purposes I cannot measure or understand. Yet I thank You for the good I know, for the life I have, and for the gifts that – in sickness and in health – have been my daily portion: the beauty of earth and sky, the visions that have stirred me from my ease and quickened my endeavours, the demands of truth and justice that move me to acts of goodness, and the contemplation of Your eternal presence, which fills me with hope that what is good and lovely cannot perish. For all this, I give thanks.

Liberal Jewish Prayer Book

27

Remembering the Dead

At this time of the year when we consider the sum of our lives it is natural to think of those who touched and enriched them, and who continue to inspire us even though they are no longer in our midst.

It is customary during this period to visit the graves of one's ancestors and relatives. It is also customary to prostrate oneself on the graves of the pious and to be liberal with supplications and with charity to the poor in the graveyard.

S. Y. Agnon

Immortality, mine, my people's, and others, refers to something indefeasible, something sacred that will not be trampled underfoot. I hope – don't we all? – to leave a shadow on this earth to offer testimony that I have lived. For all his humour the comedian may have been right in his desire to have immortality here and now. It's a question of knowing where to look for it. A legend tells of the angels who were jealous that God was to create the human being in God's own image. That image is immortal. God and his human creations would share immortality. Why, then, were Adam and Eve so anxious to eat from the tree of life – the tree of immortality – after they ate from the tree of knowledge?

Because they learned that the angels plotted to hide it from them. One angel proposed that immortality be hidden from them in the mountains or the seas far beyond the reach of man or woman. But others argued that human beings would climb the mountains and plumb the oceans to find it. Then the shrewdest angel of all suggested that immortality be hidden within and between human beings. That angel surmised that within and between would be the last place on earth people would search to discover eternal life, now that we know the secret. Immortality is within and between us, and its intimations are here and now.

Harold M. Schulweis

I had thought that your death
Was a waste and a destruction,
A pain of grief hardly to be endured.
I am only beginning to learn
That your life was a gift and a growing
And a loving left with me.
The desperation of death
Destroyed the existence of love,
But the fact of death
Cannot destroy what has been given.
I am learning to look at your life again
Instead of your death and departing.

Marjorie Pizer

The difference between the living and the dead is the difference between the remembered and the forgotten. To be alive but forgotten, or neglected, or denied: is that not a kind of death? And to be dead but remembered, or studied, or missed: is that not a kind of life?

Leon Wieseltier

Let us now praise famous men,
And our fathers that begot us.
The Lord has wrought great glory by them
Through his great power from the beginning . . .
But these were merciful men,
Whose righteousness hath not been forgotten.
With their seed shall continually remain a good inheritance,
And their children are within the covenant.
And their seed standeth fast,
And their children for their sakes.
And their seed shall remain for ever,
And their glory shall not be blotted out.
Their bodies are buried in peace;
But their name liveth for evermore.
The people will tell of their wisdom,
And the congregation will show forth their praise.

Ecclesiasticus 44.1–2, 10–15

Strange is our situation here upon earth.
Each of us comes for a short visit, not knowing why,
yet sometimes seeming to divine a purpose.
From the standpoint of daily life, however,
there is one thing we do know:
that we are here for the sake of others;
above all for those on whose smile and well-being
our own happiness depends;
and also for the countless unknown souls
with whose fate we are connected
by a bond of sympathy.

Many times a day I realise how much
my own outer and inner life is built upon the labours of
    others,
both living and dead,

and how earnestly I must exert myself
in order to give in return as much
as I have received and am still receiving.

Albert Einstein

There are stars whose radiance is visible on earth
though they have long been extinct. There are people whose
brilliance continues to light the world
though they are no longer among the living.
These lights are particularly bright when the night is dark.
They light the way for us all.

Hannah Senesh

28

Mystery

We cannot hope to penetrate the mystery of God, only to strive to live within it; at the High Holy Days we contemplate God's mystery and with it the mystery and wonder of our own existence.

I do not know your ways
For me the sun setting is
God setting.
Where do you go to
God?
Take me with you,
if in going with you
there is light,
God.
I am afraid of the dark.

Malka Heifetz Tussman

Behind every certainty there stands a concealment, behind every new clarity a new mystery is revealed. All the certainties, all the concealments, and the searching spirit itself that travelled out into them, all are embraced by something unfathomable, by the miracle of all the miracles. Behind all of them, above all of them, and beneath all of them is the great mystery which is beyond space and time, which exists through itself and which exists through everything that is. No man's mind has fathomed it or will be able to fathom it. But reverence, that reverence without which love does not live and faithfulness does not endure, may approach it. And it hears the voice out of the mystery: "I AM THAT I AM, thy God."

Leo Baeck

Indeed, it is from within immanence itself that we rediscover transcendence: God is so profoundly and ineffably present in each moment, in every place, and in a special way in each human soul that the encounter with that presence leads us right back to transcendent mystery.

Arthur Green

Gathering the Sparks
Long before the sun cast a shadow,
before the Word was spoken
that brought the heavens
and the earth
into being,
a flame emerged
from a single,
unseen
point,
and from the center of this flame
sparks of light sprang forth,
concealed in shells,
that set sail everywhere
above
and below,

like a fleet of ships
each carrying its cargo
of light.

Somehow,
no one knows why,
the frail vessels broke open,
split asunder,
and all the sparks were scattered
like sand
like seeds
like stars.

That is why we were created –
to search for the sparks
no matter where they have been
hidden,
and as each one is revealed,
to be consumed
in our own fire
and reborn
out of our own
ashes.

Someday,
when the sparks have been gathered,
the vessels will be
restored,
and the fleet will set sail
across another ocean
of space,
and the Word
will be spoken
again.

Howard Schwartz

To pray is to regain a sense of the mystery that animates all being, the divine margin in all attainments. Prayer is our humble answer to the inconceivable surprise of living. It is all we can offer in return for the mystery by which we live. Who is worthy to be present at the constant unfolding of time? Amidst the meditation of mountains, the humility of flowers – wiser than all alphabets – clouds that die constantly for the sake of His glory, we are hating, hunting, hurting. Suddenly we feel ashamed of our clashes and complaints in the face of the tacit glory in nature. It is so embarrassing to live! How strange we are in the world, and how presumptuous our doings! Only one response can maintain us: gratefulness for witnessing the wonder, for the gift of our unearned right to serve, to adore, and to fulfil. It is gratefulness which makes the soul great.

Abraham Joshua Heschel

Out of the depths of the springs of my soul,
to You, O hidden God, I cry – hear my prayer:
Demand of me what You will, O God, here am I!
Only show me Your face, let me see Your face!
Of what use are life's riches which You put all around me,
Or all the splendour of the worlds which You have put into
   my heart?
They are pale shadows of Your hidden light,
Blurred outlines of Your true image.
But I would drink of the Source of all sources,
I long to bathe in the Light of all lights –
Your face, *Your* face I crave to see.

Jacob Cahan

The Thread

Something is very gently,
invisibly, silently,
pulling at me – a thread
or net of threads
finer than cobweb and as
elastic. I haven't tried
the strength of it. No barbed hook
pierced and tore me. Was it
not long ago this thread
began to draw me? Or
way back? Was I
born with its knot about my
neck, a bridle? Not fear
but a stirring
of wonder makes me
catch my breath when I feel
the tug of it when I thought
it had loosened itself and gone.

Denise Levertov

29

Autumn is Coming

Autumn is the season of contemplation and quiet reckoning,
of endings and new beginnings.

Summer is dying in misty veils
of purple and gold;
And leaves are drowning deeply
in her blood
turning to mould.

The garden is still,
Youth's happy sounds are barely heard,
Though some may wait to watch
the sudden flight
of a migrating bird.

The heart is orphaned
and whispering showers brush the pane:
"Have you fixed your shoes,
repaired your coat,
and housed your grain?"

Chaim Nachman Bialik

On Autumn Nights

On autumn nights, unseen,
a leaf falls in the forest
and lies silent on the ground. A fish
leaps from the waters
of a stream,
and an echo of wet flapping
answers in the darkness. In the black distance
unseen horses sow hoofbeats
that slowly crumble. All this
the tired traveller hears
and trembles in his bones.

David Vogel

Existence will remain meaningless for you if you yourself do not penetrate into it with active love and if you do not in this way discover its meaning for yourself. Everything is waiting to be hallowed by you; it is waiting to be disclosed in its meaning and to be realised in it by you. For the sake of this your beginning, God created the world. God has drawn it out of the Divine Essence so that you may bring it back to God. Meet the world with the fullness of your being and you shall meet God. That God . . . accepts from your hands what you have to give to the world, is Divine mercy. If you wish to believe, love!

One who loves brings God and the world together.

Martin Buber

Softly, like a murmuring of prayer,
The trees are whispering, and the leaves
Are like a voice of lamentation in the air,
That grieves. Scarce knowing why it grieves.

The branches bow their bearded heads,
And each in blessing solemnly outspreads
Its hands – In blessing of the leaves
That sway upon their edge, ready to slip
Into the larger world, to do the business of the wind.
Then suddenly the whole tree heaves –
The wind comes, roaring, cracking his whip,
Driving them, driving them slavelike, until
Tired and beaten and helpless they lie;
Then he heaps them together, and leaves them to die.

Joseph Leftwich

I saw a white bird disappear in the black night
and I knew it wouldn't be long for the light
of my eyes in that same night.

I saw a cloud as small as my hand
and I knew, though the first ripples widen in
that pond,
that I haven't been able to make anyone
understand.

I saw a leaf that fell, a leaf is falling.
Time is short, I am not complaining.

Natan Zach

The quality of life is what counts. And that is something
which is attainable regardless of whether we are young or
old, whether we are in the spring, the summer, the autumn,
or the winter of our lives. Indeed, there is a sense in which it
does, or should become *more* attainable as we grow older. For
though we become less agile, alert and energetic, we should

become wiser, more experienced, more discriminating; better able to understand ourselves and our fellow human beings, and so to use our aptitudes and opportunities to the best advantage.

John D. Rayner

Now is the time for turning
The leaves are beginning to turn from green to red and
    orange.
The birds are beginning to turn and are heading once more
toward the south. The animals are beginning to turn to
    storing their food for the winter.
For leaves, birds, and animals, turning comes instinctively.

But for us turning does not come so easily. It takes an act
    of will for us to make a turn.

It means breaking with old habits. It means admitting that
    we have been wrong; and this is never easy. It means
    losing face; it means starting over again; and this is
    always painful. It means saying: I am sorry. It means
    recognising that we have the ability to change.

These things are terribly hard to do.
But unless we turn, we will be trapped forever in
    yesterday's ways.
God, help us to turn –
    from callousness to sensitivity
    from hostility to love
    from pettiness to purpose,
    from envy to contentment,
    from carelessness to discipline
    from fear to faith.

HIGH AND HOLY DAYS

Turn us around, O God, and bring us back toward you.
Revive our lives, as at the beginning.

And turn us toward each other, God,
for in isolation there is no life.

Jack Riemer

30

Creation

In Jewish tradition Rosh Hashanah marks the birthday of the world: we celebrate the richness and diversity of our world and resolve to play an active and responsible part in protecting and preserving it.

Then the Lord answered Job out of the whirlwind: Where were you when I laid the foundations of the earth? Tell me, if you have understanding. Who determined its measurements – surely you know! Or who stretched the line upon it? On what were its bases sunk, or who laid its cornerstone when the morning stars sang together and all the heavenly beings shouted for joy? Or who shut in the sea with doors when it burst out from the womb? – when I made the clouds its garment, and thick darkness its swaddling band, and prescribed bounds for it, and set bars and doors, and said, "Thus far shall you come and no farther, and here shall your proud waves be stopped"?

Job 38.1, 4–11

The stars of heaven, awesome in their majesty,
are not more wonderful than the one who charts their
    courses.
The elements, arrayed in perfection,

are not marvels greater than the mind that beholds them.
This miracle, matter, begets a wonder:
the body thinks, insight comes from flesh,
the soul is born of dust to build towers of hope,
opening within us doors of lamentation and love.
For You have made us little less than divine,
and crowned us with glory and honour!
Glory and honour within us:
but every age has despised its endowment.
And yet, O God, we look with hope beyond the near
    horizon.
Beneath this trampled earth
a seed for goodness will grow, we trust,
to be our tree of life.
Within and beyond us,
O God of life, You are there.
You dwell wherever we let you in.
When we flee from You, we flee from ourselves.
When we seek You, we discover that we are not alone.

Chaim Stern

The essence of the Jewish conception of life seems to me to lie
in an affirmative attitude to the life of all creation. The life of
the individual has meaning only insofar as it aids in making
the life of every living thing nobler and more beautiful. Life
is sacred – that is to say, it is the supreme value to which all
other values are subordinate. The hallowing of the supra-
individual life brings in its train a reverence for everything
spiritual – a particularly characteristic feature of the Jewish
tradition.

But the Jewish tradition also contains something else,
something which finds splendid expression in many of the
Psalms, namely a sort of intoxicated joy and amazement at

the beauty and grandeur of this world, of which humankind can just form a faint notion. It is the feeling from which true scientific research draws its spiritual substance, but which also seems to find expression in leafy trees and the crash of waves.

Albert Einstein

After the Great Maggid's death, his disciples came together and talked about the things he had done. When it was Rabbi Schneur Zalman's turn, he asked them: "Do you know why our master went to the pond every day at dawn and stayed there for a little while before coming home again?" They did not know why. Rabbi Zalman continued: "He was learning the song with which the frogs praise God. It takes a very long time to learn that song."

Martin Buber

The Sun
Have you ever seen
anything
in your life
more wonderful

than the way the sun,
every evening
relaxed and easy,
floats toward the horizon

and into the clouds or the hills,
or the rumpled sea,
and is gone –
and how it slides again

out of the blackness
every morning,
on the other side of the world,
like a red flower

streaming upward on its heavenly oils,
say, on a morning in early summer,
at its perfect imperial distance –
and have you ever felt for anything

such wild love –
do you think there is anywhere, in any language,
a word billowing enough
for the pleasure
that fills you
as the sun
reaches out,
as it warms you –

as you stand there,
empty-handed –
or have you too
turned from this world –

or have you too
gone crazy
for power,
for things?

Mary Oliver

CREATION

In the Beginning

Fellow humans, to whom a year is a long time,
A century a venerable goal,
Struggling for your bread,
Tired, fretful, tricked, sick, lost:
Listen, and may it be mockery and consolation.
Twenty billion years before now,
Brilliant, soaring in space and time,
There was a ball of flame, solitary, eternal,
Our common father and our executioner.
It exploded, and every change began.
Even now the thin echo of this one reverse catastrophe
Resounds from the farthest reaches.
From that one spasm everything was born:
The same abyss that enfolds and challenges us,
The same time that spawns and defeats us,
Everything anyone has ever thought,
The eyes of every woman we have loved,
Suns by the thousands
And this hand that writes.

Primo Levi

My thoughts awaken me to see You;
They show me Your deeds in my heart's eye;
They teach me to recount Your wonders,
   "When I behold Your heavens,
   The work of Your fingers."

Around its course the disk of heaven moves,
A potter's wheel encircling the world;
It has no lips, and yet it tells Your glory
To earth, unmoved within its orbit,
   Suspended in the void,
   Stayed by the cords of Your love.

Thither the sun yearns, and there burns,
And of its light some to the moon lends.
While heaven's sphere is spread out like a tent,
With stars blooming on it, a garden,
  Proclaiming how profound
  The plans that You have laid.

Moses ibn Ezra

31

Erev Rosh Hashanah

Out of darkness God created light. Rosh Hashanah shines light on the dark places of our lives as well as inspiring us with renewed vigour and hope for the year that lies ahead.

As we Jews now enter the High Holidays again, preparing ourselves to pray for a year of peace and happiness for our people and all people, let us make up, Master of the Universe. In spite of everything that happened? Yes, in spite. Let us make up: for the child in me, it is unbearable to be divorced from You so long.

Elie Wiesel

That life is both fleeting and uncertain is a truth that presses upon the mind with special force as the old year ends and the new begins. Time speeds on, and we go with it, and though we have seen the old year close, we can never be sure of seeing the end of the new. We are utterly in Your hands, O God. And so we are led to turn our thoughts to You, to remember that You have given us our lives in trust, to use in Your service. But since life is so fleeting and frail, we must begin this serious use of it at once, and begin it by entering upon the task of self-examination and self-ennoblement which is its essential preliminary. A New Year, say the rabbis, should inaugurate a new life.

Morris Joseph

Rosh Ha-Shanah
New Year
New Moon of *Tishri*
Dawning darkly
First stars
Sparkling pathways
From the past
Into the future

Hinneyni
Here I am
Standing on the threshold
Of the new year
Ready
But
Retreating

Teshuvah?
I turn back from the brink
Sarah's laughter
Ringing in my ears
New life?

New beginning?
Is it possible?
For me?
And then
In the desert
Of those questions
Hagar's eyes opening
Opening mine
Forcing me
To turn around again
Pressing me
To look forward
To gaze into the landscape
Beyond
To see
Wells of water
In the wilderness

Hinneyni
Here I am
Standing on the threshold
Of the new year
Ready
To begin
Again.

Elizabeth Tikvah Sarah

EREV ROSH HASHANAH

A woman and a Jew, sometimes more
of a contradiction than I can sweat out,
yet finally the intersection that is both
collision and fusion, stone and seed.

Like any poet I wrestle the holy name
and know there is no wording finally
can map, constrain or summon that fierce
voice whose long wind lifts my hair,

chills my skin and fills my lungs
to bursting. I serve the word
I cannot name, who names me daily,
who speaks me out by whispers and shouts.

Coming to the new year, I am picked
up like the ancient ram's horn to sound
over the congregation of people and beetles,
of pines, whales, marshhawks and asters.

Then I am dropped into the factory of words
to turn my little wheels and grind my own
edges, back on piece work again, knowing there is no
    justice
we don't make daily

like bread and love.

Marge Piercy

The eve of Rosh Hashanah at the house that's being built,
a man makes a vow: not to do anything wrong in it,
only to love.
Sins that were green last spring
dried out over the summer. Now they're whispering.

So I washed my body and clipped my fingernails,
the last good deed a man can do for himself
while he's still alive.

What is man? In the daytime he untangles into words
what night turns into a heavy coil.
What do we do to one another –
a son to his father, a father to his son?

And between him and death there's nothing
but a wall of words
like a battery of agitated lawyers.

And whoever uses people as handles or as rungs of a ladder
will soon find himself hugging a stick of wood
and holding a severed hand and wiping his tears
with a potsherd.

Yehuda Amichai

At the New Year

Every single instant begins another new year;
    Sunlight flashing on water, or plunging into a clearing
In quiet woods announces; the hovering gull proclaims
    Even in wide midsummer a point of turning: and fading
Late winter daylight close behind the huddled backs
    Of houses close to the edge of town flares up and
        shatters
As well as any screeching ram's horn can, wheel
    Unbroken, uncomprehended continuity.
Making a starting point of a moment along the way.
    Spinning the year about one day's pivot of change.
But if there is to be a high moment of turning
    When a great, autumnal page, say, takes up its curved
Flight in memory's spaces, and with a final sigh,

As of every door in the world shutting at once, subsides
Into the bed of its fellows; if there is to be
 A time of tallying, recounting and rereading
Illuminated annals, crowded with black and white
 And here and there a capital flaring with silver and
  bright
Blue, then let it come at a time like this, not at winter's
Night, when a few dead leaves crusted with frost lie
  shivering
On our doorsteps to be counted, or when our moments of
  coldness
 Rise up to chill us again. But let us say at a golden
Moment just on the edge of harvesting, "Yes. Now."
 Times of counting are times of remembering; here amidst
  showers
Of shiny fruits, both the sweet and the bitter-tasting results,
 The honey of promises gleams on apples that turn to
  mud
In our innermost of mouths, we can sit facing westward
 Toward imminent rich tents, telling and remembering.
Not like merchants with pursed hearts, counting in dearth
  and darkness,
 But as when from a shining eminence, someone walking
  starts
At the sudden view of imperturbable blue on one hand
 And wide green fields on the other. Not at the reddening
  sands
Behind, nor yet at the blind gleam, ahead, of something
 Golden, looking at such a distance and in such sunlight,
Like something given – so, at this time, our counting
  begins,
 Whirling all its syllables into the circling wind
That plays about our faces with a force between a blow's
 And a caress', Like the strength of a blessing, as we go

Quietly on with what we shall be doing, and sing
   Thanks for being enabled, again, to begin this instant.

John Hollander

With what shall I approach the Eternal One?
How shall I worship the God of heaven?
Shall I come before God with burnt-offerings
or with yearling calves?

Will God be pleased with thousands of rams,
or with ten thousand rivers of oil?
Should I give my first-born for my transgressions,
the fruit of my body for the sins of my soul?

People tell you what is good,
but what does the Eternal One require of you?
Only to do justly,
and love mercy,
and walk humbly with your God.

Micah 6.6–8

32

Rosh Hashanah

The Jewish New Year is not an occasion for extremes, either for unbridled celebration or seeking to blot out the misery or misdeeds of the past; rather it is the time when we contemplate our actions and in so doing resolve to improve ourselves in the year ahead.

The God of judgement stands for conscience; *Rosh Hashanah* becomes a time for self-examination and commitment to growth and change of habits. The essential statement of faith is that we *are* capable of change. God calls upon us, symbolically through this season but actually at all times, to be the best human beings, morally and spiritually, that we can be. This demands of us a constant openness to change and growth.

Arthur Green

'Remember us for life! O Sovereign who delights in life.' We repeat this prayer throughout the High Holydays. In the year gone by, did we fill our days with the kind of life that delights the Sovereign? Did we waste our days in the year gone by? Did we value the treasure of life? Did we appreciate our family and friends? Did we flee from others, from ourselves, from God? And what will we do with a new year?

Jules Harlow

It is out of kindness towards human beings that God remembers us and reviews our deeds year after year on Rosh Hashanah, that our sins may not grow too numerous; that there may be room for forgiveness; that, our sins being few, God may forgive them. For this reason, it is fitting that we celebrate Rosh Hashanah as a festive day; but since it is a Day of Judgement for all living things, it is also fitting that we observe it with greater awe and reverence than all the other festive days.

Sefer ha-Chinnuch

This is the autumn and our harvest –
such as it is, such as it is –
the beginnings of the end, bare trees and barren ground;
but for us only the beginning:
let the wild goat's horn
and the silver trumpet sound!

Reason upon reason
to be thankful:
for the fruit of the earth,
for the fruit of the tree,
for the light of the fire,
and to have come to this season.

You have loved us greatly and given us
Your laws
for an inheritance,
Your Sabbaths, holidays, and seasons of gladness,
distinguishing Israel
from other nations –
distinguishing us
above the shoals of men.
And yet why should we be remembered –

if at all – only for peace, if grief
is also for all? Our hopes,
if they blossom, if they blossom at all, the petals
and fruit fall.

You have given us the strength
to serve You,
but we may serve or not
as we please;
not for peace nor for prosperity,
not even for length of life, have we merited
remembrance; remember us
as the servants
You have inherited.

Charles Reznikoff

Footnote to a Rosh Hashanah Prayer
Like the rays of the late afternoon sun
Slanting through the trees, shining on each separate leaf,
You shine on us, our God,
And like the leaves we reflect Your light.

I thank You with all my heart
For the presence of Your spirit, which is life.
I pray You not to withdraw from me,
I pray You not to depart from me, though I am unworthy,
I pray You let me pray to You.

How can I love you, who are so far away?
How can I know You, whose face I have not seen?
How can I approach You, when I am laden with guilt?

I can love some of Your creatures, and so love something
    of You.

I can know some of Your world, and so know something
   of You.
I can approach You with repentance and prayer and
   righteous deeds,
But I can do none of these, my God, without Your help.

Help me love You and know You and pray to You
That this my existence may become a life,
A life that like a leaf in the afternoon sun
Reflects Your great and golden light.

Ruth F. Brin

A Kavanah for Rosh Hashanah
In your mercy help us, Adonai,
to embrace Your sacred gift
of Rosh Hashanah
in love and in joy.
May the holiness of this day
bring fullness to our faith in You.
Help us to gather
all those scattered sparks of faith
which are lost within ourselves,
as Your people Israel
gather in congregations
everywhere
to praise Your name
this day.

Nachman of Bratzlav

One year Reb Levi Yitzchak of Berditchev spent a long
time in search of a man who would be worthy of blowing
the shofar in his *beis midrash*. Rosh Hashanah was fast

approaching, and though many righteous folk sought the privilege, vying with each other in demonstrating their expertise in the abstruse kabbalistic secrets associated with the shofar, none of them were to his taste.

One day a new applicant came along, and Reb Levi Yitzchak asked him on what dread mysteries he meditated while he was performing the awesome mitzvah.

"Rebbe," said the newcomer, "I'm only a simple fellow; I don't understand too much about the hidden things of the Torah. But I have four daughters of marriageable age, and when I blow the shofar, this is what I have in mind: 'The Master of the Universe! Right now I am carrying out Your will. I'm doing Your mitzvah and blowing the shofar. Now supposing You too do what I want, and help me marry off my daughters?'"

"My friend," said Reb Levi Yitzchak, "you will blow the shofar in my synagogue!"

S. Y. Zevin

33

The Shofar

The unique ritual of Rosh Hashanah is the multiple sounding of the ram's horn. It is a reminder of the ram sacrificed in place of Isaac, whose story we read on this day. The mysterious sound of this most primitive instrument takes us back to the dawn of our people's journey through history.

The ram's horn cut off
to proclaim the brokenness
of the heart,
only what's incomplete
may sound the yearning
to be whole.

Israel Zoberman

Once, when Rabbi Bunam honoured a man in his House of Prayer by asking him to blow the ram's horn, and the fellow began to make lengthy preparations to concentrate on the meaning of the sounds, the *tzaddik* cried out: "Fool, go ahead and blow!"

Martin Buber

The mystics have their own interpretation of the Shofar; they use the illustration of a lover serenading his beloved. Israel seeks to awaken the divine love and to link the higher and lower worlds. Others speak of the Shofar sounds as a prayer without words. There is a longing in the human soul too deep to be conveyed in speech, which finds expression in the yearning notes of the Shofar. The Shofar, the wind instrument, is further said to symbolise the spiritual side of life. (In Hebrew the word *ruach* means both "wind" and "spirit"). On Rosh Hashanah, we should be aware of the demands of the spirit in the year ahead and thus awaken our higher mercies.

Modern Jewish thinkers have given their interpretations of the Shofar. One of the finest of these is Milton Steinberg's exposition that the Shofar is a call to us to hear the sound of weeping humanity, to feel what the poet calls the *Weltschmerz*, the unspeakable pain of the world, and to resolve to do battle against all those forces working for humanity's oppression and subjugation, to the end that the day might come when the tear is wiped from every cheek and the sigh from every lip.

Louis Jacobs

Rabbi Pinchas Shapiro, the Koretzer Rebbe, once sat and struggled with a passage from the prophet Isaiah: "It is written, 'Lift up thy voice as a shofar'" (Isaiah 58.1).

"What could it mean?" he wondered. "How can a voice become like a shofar?"

After pondering the verse further, Rabbi Pinchas suddenly realised that God was revealing to us something about the nature of prayer.

"The Shofar remains silent," he said, "and cannot emit a sound unless the breath of a person passes through it. When we become like a shofar, the breath of the Holy One, the divine Shechinah, passes through us. That is how we pray: the breath of God's Indwelling Presence vibrates on our lips. We may think we pray to God, but that is not exactly so: the prayer itself is divine."

David Patterson

The fat time of the year is also time
Of the Atonement; birds to the berry bushes,
Men to the harvest; a time to answer for
Both present plenty and emptiness to come.
When the slain legal deer is salted down,
When apples smell like goodness, cold in the cellar,
You hear the ram's horn sounded in the high
Mount of the Lord, and you lift up your eyes
As though by this observance you might hide
The dry husk of an eaten heart which brings
Nothing to offer up, no sacrifice
Acceptable but the cancelled-out desires
And satisfactions of another year's
Abscess, whose zero in His winter's mercy
Still hides the undecipherable seed.

Howard Nemerov

The Shofar Calls
The shofar calls: Tekiah
   Arise! Awake! From your beds, your homes
   to the blast that calls you,
   the siren that warns you:
   seek shelter for your spirit,
   enter now the opening gates.

THE SHOFAR

The ram's horn cries: Shevarim
    Worship in truth, pray together
    in confidence and in trust,
    determined that promises shall be kept,
    oaths fulfilled, words spoken thoughtfully
    in honour and in truth.

The shrill notes tremble: Teruah
    Listen to the cries of the ancient martyrs,
    sense the unbearable silence of the dead,
    contemplate in reverence and awe
    all those who died "L'kiddush ha-Shem".

The shofar blasts: Tekiah gadolah
    Remember! Recall the ages of our people,
    Dwell on your own life in the year that has passed,
    Call up from the darkness the mistakes, the errors,
    the evil deeds that you must deal with now.

Three times three the great horn blows: Tekiah, shevarim,
    teruah
    Return! Return to God Who made you,
    Arise to prayer, awake to memory, achieve repentance.
    Return to God Who loves you,
    Now while the days of awe are passing,
    before the closing of the gates.

Ruth F. Brin

From year to year the need becomes more urgent for a religion that teaches reverence for life as its highest principle. Judaism is such a religion. The God it worships does not desire the death of sinners, but that they may turn and live: God's word is "Seek me and live" and "Choose life". Judaism is a religion which teaches that to destroy a single life is to destroy an entire world, and to sustain a single life is to sustain an entire world. It is a religion that yearns, above all things, for the day when swords will be beaten into plough-shares and spears into pruninghooks; whose aim, in the words of a modern Jewish writer, is "the creation of a human being unable to shed blood"; whose toast is *Lechayyim*, "To life!"

It is the religion of the *Akedah*, which is a symbol of life, not death, because Abraham is forbidden to sacrifice his son. It is a religion whose New Year is a celebration of life and a plea for its continuance: "Remember us unto life, O Sovereign who delights in life, and inscribe us in the book of Life, for Your sake, O God of life."

John D. Rayner

34

Tashlich

On the afternoon of Rosh Hashanah there is a folk custom of gathering by a river or the sea and casting crumbs into the water to symbolize the casting away of one's sins. It is a reminder of the ritual of the scapegoat of biblical times, a physical rite by which even our secret sins are transferred and discarded.

Taschlich is a communal as well as a private act. We go together to a body of water in a spirit of humility, self-scrutiny and desire for renewal. Together we recite prayers that acknowledge our sins and request divine forgiveness. Then as individuals we reach into our pockets, scattering the accumulated dust and crumbs they contain upon the waters, symbolically casting our sins away.

Editors

God, I know that the wrongs I have done are too many to
    be told, and my faults too many to recall.
Nevertheless, I shall recall some of them and confess,
    though they are like a drop from the ocean.
Perhaps I can calm their uproar and tumult, like the waves
    and breakers of the sea, and You will listen and forgive.

Anon

Let us cast away the sin of deception,
so that we will mislead no one in word or deed,
nor pretend to be what we are not.

Let us cast away the sin of vain ambition,
which prompts us to strive for goals
that bring neither true fulfilment nor genuine contentment.

Let us cast away the sin of stubbornness,
so that we will neither persist in foolish habits
nor maintain our unwillingness to change.

Let us cast away the sin of selfishness,
which keeps us from enriching our lives
through wider concerns and greater sharing,
and from reaching out in love to our fellow human beings.

Let us cast away the sin of indifference,
so that we may become more sensitive to the sufferings of
    others
and responsive to the needs of people everywhere.

Let us cast away the sins of pride and arrogance,
so that we can worship God
and serve God's purposes in humility and truth.

Jonathan Cohen

It was Rosh Hashanah and I put on the new gabardine
and new shoes I had been given and brushed my sidelocks
behind my ears. What more could a young Chassid do to
look modern? In the late afternoon I started to loiter on
Bridge Street, watching the townspeople file by on their way
to the Tashlich ceremony. The day was sunny, the sky as
blue and transparent as it is in mid-summer. Cool breezes
mingled with the warmth exuded by the earth. First came
the Chassidim, marching together as a group, all dressed in

fur hats and satin coats. They hurried along as if they were rushing from their womenfolk and temptation. I had been raised among these people, but now I found their dishevelled beards, their ill-fitting clothes and their insistent clannishness odd. They ran from the Evil One like sheep from a wolf. After the Chassidim came the ordinary Jews, and after them the women and girls . . .

Some of the townspeople stood on the wooden bridge reciting the Tashlich; others lined the river's banks. Young women took out their handkerchiefs and shook out their sins. Boys playfully emptied their pockets to be sure that no transgression remained. The village wits made the traditional Tashlich jokes. "Girls, shake as hard as you want, but a few sins will remain." "The fish will get fat feeding on so many errors . . ."

Suddenly I felt a tug at my sleeve, I turned and trembled. Feigele stood next to me. So great was my amazement that I forgot to marvel. She wore a black suit, a black beret, and a white lace collar. Her face lit by the setting sun shone with Rosh Hashanah purity. "Excuse me," she said. "Can you locate the Tashlich for me? I can't seem to find the place." Her smile seemed to be saying. "Well, this was the best pretext available". . . She held in her hand a prayer book which had covers stamped in gold. I took one cover of the book and she grasped the other. I started to turn the pages. On one side of the page was Hebrew and on the other Polish: I kept turning the leaves but couldn't find the prayer either . . .

The prayer seemed to have flown from the book. But I knew it was there and that my eyes had been bewitched. I was just about to give up looking when I saw the word "Tashlich" printed in big bold letters. "Here it is," I cried out, and my heart seemed to stop.

"What? Thank you."

"I haven't recited the Tashlich myself," I said.

"Well, suppose we say it together."

"Can you read Hebrew script?"

"Of course."

"This prayer symbolizes the casting of one's sins into the ocean."

"Naturally."

We stood muttering the prayer together as the crowd slowly moved off . . .

Isaac Bashevis Singer

Out of the depths I call to you, Eternal One.
Hear my voice, Adonai,
let your ears be attentive
to my plea.

If you kept account of sins, Eternal One,
Adonai, who could survive?
For with you there is forgiveness
that you may be held in awe.

I wait for the Eternal One, my whole being waits,
I await God's word.
My soul yearns for Adonai more eagerly
than the morning watchmen watch for the dawn.

O Israel, wait for the Eternal One
for with the Eternal there is steadfast love
and great powers to redeem.
God shall redeem Israel
from all its iniquities.

Psalm 130

TASHLICH

This afternoon my family and I will drive to the beach to perform the ancient ritual of *tashlich*. Like so many Jews before us, we will gather at the water's edge and empty our pockets. We will cast out the crumbs of last year's deeds, the memories of wounds sustained and inflicted, the remnants of conversations that hurt instead of healed. Standing on the shore of the ocean, we will repeat some ancient words and add some of our own, grateful to the Source of Life who enables us to distinguish between what must be cast off and what must be cherished and preserved. On this day of remembering, we shall remember. On this day of judgment, we will seek to become bringers of justice. On this day of listening, we will try very hard to listen to the still, small voice that inspires us toward acts of loving-kindness. And through such acts each of us can save the world.

Sue Levi Elwell

Help us to return to You, O God, then we shall return. Renew our days as in the past.

Lamentations 5.21

35

Community

The prayers recited during the High Holy Days are always couched in the plural: though we pray as individuals, we gain support from those around us praying the same prayers but with their own unique voice.

We Jews are a community based on memory. A common memory has kept us together and enabled us to survive. This does not mean that we based our life on any one particular past, even on the loftiest of pasts; it simply means that one generation passed on to the next a memory which gained in scope – for new destiny and new emotional life were constantly accruing to it – and which realised itself in a way we can call organic. This expanding memory was more than a spiritual motif; it was a power which sustained, fed, and quickened Jewish existence itself.

Martin Buber

Suppose there are several people in a boat, and one of them takes a drill, and starts to bore a hole, and the others protest: 'What are you doing?' If the one drilling answers: 'What business is it of yours? Am I not boring under my own self?', surely they will retort: 'But it *is* our business, because when the water comes in, it will sink the boat with all of us in it!'

Midrash

We Jews have a more pressing responsibility for our lives and beliefs than perhaps any other religious community.

Don't shelter yourself in any course of action by the idea that 'it is my affair'. It is your affair, but it is also mine and the community's. Nor can we neglect the world beyond. A fierce light beats down upon the Jew. It is a grave responsibility this – to be a Jew; and you can't escape from it, even if you choose to ignore it. Ethically or religiously, we Jews can be and do nothing light-heartedly. Ten bad Jews may help to damn us; ten good Jews may help to save us. Which *minyan* will you join?

Claude G. Montefiore

If you think you can live without others, you are mistaken, and you are even more mistaken if you think others cannot live without you.

Chaim Stern

A Talmudic adage urges, *tafasta m'rubah lo tafasta*, "if you reach too far you capture nothing". The successful beginning, then, is hardly a mission statement announcing the need to find God in an instant, or even a day, or a month, or a year. Sacred community begins with a modest but firm commitment to the project of our generation: to transcend ethnicity and seek out the holy in such things as the ways we think, the blessings we say, the truths we discover, and the homes we have or seek to find. Jewish spirituality is not just real. It is reasonable and it is deep. And it beckons us now more than ever to return home to find it.

Lawrence A. Hoffman

Once, the Baal Shem stood in the House of Prayer and prayed for a very long time. All his disciples had finished praying, but he continued without paying any attention to them. They waited for him a good while, and then they went home. After several hours when they had attended to their various duties, they returned to the House of Prayer and found him still deep in prayer. Later, he said to them: "By going away and leaving me alone, you dealt me a painful separation. I shall tell you a parable.

"You know that there are birds of passage who fly to warm countries in the autumn. Well, the people in one of those lands once saw a glorious many-coloured bird in the midst of a flock which was journeying through the sky. The eyes of man had never seen a bird so beautiful. He alighted on the top of the tallest tree and nested in the leaves. When the king of the country heard of it, he bade them fetch down the bird with his nest. He ordered a number of men to make a ladder up the tree. One was to stand on the others' shoulders until it was possible to reach up high enough to take the nest. It took a long time to build this living ladder. Those who stood nearest the ground lost patience, shook themselves free, and everything collapsed."

Martin Buber

God says: "If you occupy yourself with the study of Torah, perform acts of kindness, and pray with the community, I consider you as if you had redeemed Me and My children.

To occupy oneself with the needs of the community is as much a religious act as to study Torah.

May the One who blessed our ancestors bless all who occupy themselves with the needs of the community in faithfulness.

Those who share in the troubles of the community shall share in its consolation.

Mishnah

36

Tzedakah

A much-repeated prayer in the High Holy Day liturgy declares that 'Prayer, Repentance, and Charity annul the severity of the judgment'. As well as our spiritual efforts we must, if we wish to be forgiven, show charity and kindness to those less fortunate than ourselves.

It says in the Talmud: "*Gemilut chesed* is greater than charity, since charity is performed with one's money, while *chesed* is exercised both with one's money and his person." ("With one's money" here includes lending cash, articles, or livestock. *Gemilut chesed* both with one's money and his person – delivering a eulogy over the dead; acting as pall bearer; bring joy to bride and groom; escorting one's neighbour on his journey – [Rashi]). Charity is given to the poor; *gemilut chesed* is extended to poor and rich alike; charity is given to the living, *chesed* both to the living and the dead. Nevertheless charity is superior to *gemilut chesed* in several respects. Charity is an outright gift, while a *gemilut chesed* loan is advanced for a limited period after which the lender recovers his money. More effort is required to overcome one's *yetzer hara* in giving charity since one's net worth is thereby reduced (which is not so in *gemilut chesed*), and according to the effort is the reward.

Chafetz Chaim

One can always find warm hearts who in a glow of emotion would like to make the whole world happy but who have never attempted the sober experiment of bringing a real blessing to a single human being. It is easy to revel enthusiastically in one's love of man, but it is more difficult to do good to someone solely because he is a human being. When we are approached by a human being demanding his right, we cannot replace definite ethical action by mere vague good will. How often has the mere love of one's neighbour been able to compromise and hold its peace!

All love of man, if it is not to be mere unfruitful sentimentality, must have its roots in the ethical and social will, in the inner recognition of man, in the vital respect of his right – in what is meant by *Tzedakah*. That is the primary and fundamental, alone making a clear and irrefutable demand which admits of no evasion.

Leo Baeck

My God, help me become a "giver".
Help me give . . . and go on giving.
You've called on us
to be charitable;
show me how.
Show me how to give
with a pure heart,
with an open heart,
with a heart filled with joy.
Lead me to those
who are truly deserving,
for giving is so holy an act.
Help me find the truly needy,
and help them find me.

Nachman of Bratzlav

Rabbi Yehuda used to say:
Ten strong things were created in the world –
A mountain is strong, but iron cuts through it.
Iron is strong, but fire causes it to bubble.
Fire is strong, but water extinguishes it.
Water is strong, but clouds contain it.
Clouds are strong, but the wind (*ruach*) scatters them.
Breath (*ruach*) is strong, but the body holds it in.
The body is strong, but fear breaks it.
Fear is strong, but wine dissipates its effects.
Wine is strong, but sleep overcomes its power.
Death is harder than all of them.
But Tzedakah saves from death, as it is written,
"And Tzedakah saves from death". (Proverbs 10.2)

Danny Siegel

Our rabbis have taught: We support the poor of the gentiles as well as the poor of Israel, and visit the sick of the gentiles as well as the sick of Israel, and bury the poor of the gentiles as well as the dead of Israel, in the interests of peace.

Talmud

There are four types among those who give tzedakah: one who wants to give but does not want others to give – he begrudges the mitzvah to fellow human beings. One who wants others to give but does not himself give – he begrudges the mitzvah to himself. One who wants to give and wants others to give – this is a saintly person. One who does not want others to give and does not give himself – this is a scoundrel.

Mishnah

There are eight degrees of charity, each one higher than the other. The highest of all is to help the needy with a gift or loan or partnership or by enabling them to find employment so that they may become independent. The second best is to give in such a way that the giver does not know who the recipient is, and the recipient does not know the giver. That is followed by the case in which the recipient knows the giver, but the giver does not know the recipient. Next comes those who give before being asked. After them, those who give only when asked. Then those who give less than they should, but cheerfully. And lastly, those who give grudgingly.

Moses Maimonides

37

Sin

An awareness of the sins we have committed in the past year and a renewed determination to try and avoid them in the future is the core task of the High Holy Days.

At first, sin is like a spider's web; in the end, it becomes like the rope of a ship.
At first, it is like a visitor; in the end, it becomes the owner of the house.

Midrash

Eternal God, let our prayers come before you and do not hide yourself from our supplications, for we are neither so obstinate nor so insolent as to say before you, Sovereign God of our mothers and fathers, that we are righteous and have not sinned. Rather do we admit that we and our ancestors have sinned.

Machzor

A Vocabulary of Sin
Cheyt חטא is the most common word for sin, but in Biblical Hebrew, and in the prayerbook, there are three common words for sin. Often they are used synonymously, but in essence they have different meanings.

Pesha פשע means rebellion. It refers to the attitude of mind where a person sets him or herself as sole judge of their actions, recognising neither God nor God's Law, nor the civil law. For this person there are no external standards of right or wrong. Whatever pleases them or furthers their aim, it is right; whatever would frustrate their actions or displeases them, is wrong.

Avon עון means "to be twisted" or "crooked". An inherent or developed trait in the character that seems to impel the person to do wrong, to be deflected from the paths that would otherwise be considered right.

Cheyt חטא is the weakest term. It means "to miss the mark". It is used of an archer where arrows fail to hit the target. *Cheyt* is the occasion where a person has no real intention of doing wrong, but just strays from the right path or action. The careless driver, the over-indulgent or neglectful parent, the thoughtless child, all are guilty of *cheyt*. Blame is attached even to unwitting sin if it could have been avoided with the exercise of greater care.

The rabbis generally speak of sin as *Aveyrah* עברה: the opposite of *mitzvah*, the good deed, obeying God's commandment. *Aveyrah* comes from the root meaning "to pass over" – passing over the line of what is right, it is a transgression against God's law.

Louis Jacobs

Say to the House of Israel: You have been saying, "Because our transgressions and sins weigh upon us, we waste away; how can we survive?" Tell them: As I live, says the Eternal God, I do not desire the death of the wicked, but that they may turn from their way and live. Turn back, turn back

from your evil ways; for why should you choose to die, O
House of Israel?

Ezekiel 33.10–11

My God, I know my transgressions have swelled
   and my sins are beyond calibration;
but I bring them to mind, like a drop in the sea –
   confessing and hoping
to quiet the noise of the waves
   and the breakers against their reefs,
that you in the heavens will hear and forgive me.

For I've gone against your teaching,
   and held your commandments in scorn;
my mouth has come to detest them,
and too often I've uttered blasphemy –
   and been perverse and lawless;
   fractious and full of violence;
I've lied and counselled evil – deceived, scoffed and
     rebelled;

been scornful, perverse and intransigent,
   stubborn, harsh and senseless;
I've cut off your reproach and been cruel.
I've committed abominable acts
   and wandered from my path;
I've strayed from your way and instruction,
   and denied the truth you instilled.

Solomon ibn Gabirol

Ribbono shel olam
I hereby forgive
Whoever has hurt me
And whoever has done me any wrong,

Whether deliberately or accidentally,
Whether physically, financially or emotionally,
Whether by word or by deed.

May no one be punished on my account.
May it be Your will,
Eternal One my God and God of my ancestors,
That I sin no more,
That I do not revert to my old ways,
Nor anger You any more with my actions,
Nor do that which is evil in Your sight.

Wipe away my sins
With Your great compassion
Rather than through sickness or suffering.
May these words of my mouth
And the prayers that are in my heart
Be acceptable before You, O God,
My Rock and my Redeemer.

Abraham Danzig

We have offended and betrayed;
we have robbed and slandered;
we have been perverse and corrupt, arrogant and violent;
we have deceived and misled others;
we have lied and scoffed;
we have been rebellious, cynical and stubborn;
we have cheated and transgressed;
we have oppressed;
we have been obstinate, vicious and destructive;
we have acted shamefully;
we have gone astray and led others astray.

Machzor

38

Repentance

The Hebrew for repentance is *teshuvah*, which literally means "returning". *Teshuvah* is the principal aim of the High Holy Days, to turn ourselves from the wrong path and towards God and godly ways.

Not only do we fail to prepare for these days (of Awe) but we have far too limited an understanding of their potential. Our traditional conception of teshuvah is saying sorry to those we have wronged. We make our relationships with them whole again. We return a certain equilibrium to our community. But teshuvah can also be a transformational experience which makes us realise the impact of our most banal actions. Maimonides, the Rambam, describes the mental state we should adopt in approaching this process. We should think of ourselves and the world as perfectly balanced: exactly **half** guilty and **half** innocent. If we commit one sin we press down the scale of guilt against ourselves and the entire world and cause its destruction. And if we perform one good deed we press down the scale of merit and bring salvation to the entire world. Our simplest acts become infused with profound meaning.

Deborah E. Lipstadt

There are times when penitence comes suddenly. A sudden flash of spiritual awareness confronts the soul. All at once we become conscious of the evil and the sordidness of sin and are converted into new people. And in the same instant, we feel a profound relaxation within us. Such penitence is a token of some special grace, the influence of some great soul force, whose ways are to be traced to the ultimate mystery of our being.

Abraham Isaac Kook

An ignorant villager, having heard it is a good religious deed to eat and drink on the day before Yom Kippur, drank himself into a stupor. He awoke late at night, too late for Kol Nidrei services. Not knowing the prayers by heart, he devised a plan. He repeated the letters of the alphabet over and over, beseeching the Almighty to arrange them into the appropriate words of the prayers. The following day he attended the Kotzker synagogue. After Neilah, the rabbi summoned him to inquire the cause of his absence at Kol Nidrei. The villager confessed his transgression and asked whether his manner of reciting the prayers could be pardoned. The rabbi responded: "Your prayer was more acceptable than mine because you uttered it with the entire devotion of your heart."

Louis I. Newman

What is the meaning of the word "teshuvah"? What is the exact etymological significance of the term? In the Bible, the word bears a specific connotation: "at the return of the year" (2 Samuel 2.1) that is at the termination of the year's cycle. The word also appears in the following context (1 Samuel 7.15–17): "And Samuel judged Israel all the days of his life. And he went from year to year in circuit to Beth-el and Gilgal and Mizpah." "Teshuvah", repentance, signifies circular motion. When one finds oneself on the circumference of a large circle, it sometimes seems that the starting point is becoming farther and farther removed, but actually it is getting closer and closer. "At the return of the year", on Rosh Hashanah, a new calendar year begins, and with every passing day one gets farther and farther away from the starting point, the New Year. But every passing day is also a return, a drawing near to the completion of the year's cycle, the Rosh Hashanah of the next year.

Joseph B. Soloveitchik

Father, King
Every gate is locked except the gate of tears.
Beloved Lord God, hear our prayers.
Collect our tears in Your vessel,
And rescue Your people, Israel.
Father, King

May our tears wash away our sins.
You are our Father and we Your children.
All that You are is beloved by us.
Beloved Father, do not abandon Your children.
Father, King

We are aware of all You have done for us
Through Your great mercy.
There is no other to whom we should turn.
Beloved Lord God, hear us soon.
Father, King

Beloved God, You sit in judgment.
May You give great consideration to Your poor sheep.
May Your severity give way to compassion,

So that we may soon be discharged.
Father, King

Beloved Lord God, no one can escape from You.
You can find everyone,
But he who has strayed can repent.
May God accept our prayer.
Father, King

[If ever You wish to know who wrote this song,
It was Toybe, wife of Jacob Pan who created it,
Daughter of Leyb Pitsker of beloved memory.
May God protect us all.]
Father, King

Toybe Pan

The power of repentance overcomes sins of the most heinous and otherwise unforgivable character. The following is explicit that no sin overwhelms the transformative power of repentance:

A Tanna taught: Naaman was a resident alien; Neburzaradan was a righteous proselyte; descendants of Haman learnt the Torah in Bnai Brak; descendants of Sisera taught children in Jerusalem; descendants of Sennacherib gave public expositions of the Torah. Who were these? Shemaya and Abtalion.

Shemayah and Abtalion are represented as the masters of Hillel and Shammai, who founded the houses dominant in many areas of the halakhah set forth in the Mishnah and related writings. The act of repentance transforms the heirs of the destroyers of Israel and the Temple into the framers of the redemptive Oral Torah. A more extreme statement of the power of any attitude or action defies imagining – even the fact of our own day that a distant cousin of Adolph Hitler has converted to Judaism and serves in the reserves of the Israel Defence Army.

Jacob Neusner

Do not think that people are obliged to repent only for transgressions involving acts, such as sexual immorality, robbery and theft. Just as individuals must turn in repentance from such acts, so must they personally search out their evil thoughts and turn in repentance from anger, from hatred, from jealousy, from mocking thoughts, from over-concern with money or prestige, and from gluttony. From all these thoughts a person must turn in repentance. They are more serious than transgressions involving acts, for when a person is addicted to them, it is difficult to give them up. Thus it is said: "Let the wicked forsake their way, the unrighteous their thoughts."

Moses Maimonides

39

Kol Nidrei

The Eve of Yom Kippur is considered by many Jews as the holiest night of the year. Candles are lit, the fast day begins, the Torah scrolls are draped in white, and worshippers are gathered in synagogue. Then the opening invocation, Kol Nidrei, sung to a haunting melody, sets the mood for the day to come.

The whole world of the Holy One is magnificent and holy. In the holy land, the Land of Israel, the holiest city is Jerusalem. In ancient Jerusalem the holiest place was the Temple and the holiest place in the Temple was the Holy of Holies.

Among all people in the world the Jews are bound to the Land of Israel. The holiest group among the Jews was the tribe of the Levites. The holiest of the Levites were the priests and among them the holiest was the High Priest.

The holiest of all things written in the holy tongue of Hebrew is the Torah. The holiest part of the Torah is the Ten Commandments, and the holiest word in the Ten Commandments is God's Divine Name.

In all the year the holiest days are the holidays. The holiness of the Sabbath surpasses that of the holidays, and the holiest Sabbath is Yom Kippur, the Sabbath of Sabbaths.

Once each year these four supreme holinesses – of place, people, language and time – were joined. On Yom Kippur, the High Priest entered the Holy of Holies and uttered God's Divine Name. And as this moment was holy and awesome beyond human conception, it held great potential danger for the High Priest and for the Jewish people, for had the High Priest met with an obstacle at that time, through a wayward or sinful thought which could lead his mind astray, for example, the entire world hanging in the balance under judgment could have been destroyed.

Wherever a man stands with his heart directed to heaven is a Holy of Holies. Every day in a person's life is like Yom Kippur. Every Jew is a High Priest. And every word spoken in purity and holiness is God's Divine Name. Every destructive thought that we nurture, every moral catastrophe, could cause the whole world to collapse.

Sh. Ansky

Yom Kippur Eve
On the eve of Yom Kippur,
we sailed
from experiences ended to experiences begun.
The eve of Yom Kippur was for us
the beginning of time
in the silence of an island
whose candles lit the sea.
There you held me to your sorrowing heart
in the presence of the Almighty,
before you went to pray with all the rest,
before you became one of the flock
in the chapel,

one of the trees
in the forest.

Zelda Mishkofsky

Sin and Repentance

Help us, O our Father, on this solemn night, to utilise the
rites and forms for achieving a deeper insight.
Help us to discern our errors as Thou wouldst have us
discern them.
Show us that we sin against Thee when we make the lives
of others unhappy,
When our actions give needless pain and grief.
We sin when we domineer, and compel others to do only
our will,
When we suppress the souls of others for our vanity or
comfort.
We sin when we respect the wealthy without character, or
despise the poor because they are poor,
When we set ourselves up as exemplars of virtue, though
we be blameworthy.
We sin when we pervert truth, take a bribe, deal
dishonestly,
When we permit the guilty to go unchecked, and the
innocent to languish behind prison bars.
We sin when we are indifferent to the plight of our
neighbours, and seek only our own welfare,
When we make our cities a jungle, and make violence the
law.
We sin when we scoff at goodness and deride hope,
When we ridicule ideals and belittle heroism.

We sin when we permit ourselves to be ignorant people.

We sin when we act in a way to bring shame upon the
household of Israel,
When we bring down contempt upon all Jews by our
dishonesty or vulgarity.
These are the sins we have committed, and these we seek to
uproot.
Only by earnest repentance can we tear them from our
habits and our thoughts.
But this is not our first Yom Kippur, nor our first resolve to
repent.
Each year we speak the words and then resume our
wonted ways.
Give us the moral strength, O God, to break through the
vicious circle of meaningless resolutions.
Help us this time to root out degrading habits.
May this night and the coming day leave us the better for
their having been spent by us in common worship.
May the influence of this day abide with us and bring us
to true repentance.

Mordecai M. Kaplan

The Eternal One spoke to Moses, saying: Note, the tenth day
of this seventh month is the Day of Atonement. It shall be
sacred for you: you shall practise self-denial; you shall do no
work throughout that day. For it is a Day of Atonement on
which expiation is made on your behalf before the Eternal
your God.

Leviticus 23.26–28

It is forbidden to offer prayers to God in a melancholy spirit.
One should pray as a servant who ministers to his Maker
with great joy, otherwise the soul is powerless to receive

the higher illumination which prayer draws down from above. It is only fitting for the worshipper to be sad when confessing his sins but during other parts of the service no sad thoughts should be present, even concern about the sins he has committed. Truly it is good for the worshipper to be in a humble frame of mind but a very joyful one. This is an exceedingly great principle of which it is proper to take note.

Isaac Luria

Once, just before New Year's, the Baal Shem came to a certain town and asked the people, who led the prayers there during the Days of Awe. They replied that this was done by the *rav* of the town. "And what is his manner of praying?" asked the Baal Shem.

"On the Day of Atonement," they said, "he recites all the confessions of sin in the most cheerful tones."

The Baal Shem sent for the *rav* and asked him the cause of this strange procedure. The *rav* answered: "The least among the servants of the king, he whose task is to sweep the forecourt free of dirt, sings a merry song as he works, for he does what he is doing to gladden the king."

Said the Baal Shem: "May my lot be with yours."

Martin Buber

Erev Yom Kippur
I lay my pain upon Your altar, loving God;
This is my lamb, my ram, my sacrifice,

My plea for pardon, plea for forgiveness
For all my sins of doing and not doing,

Prayers that blossom like flowers out of pain
Above the earth-pull.

My people's pains have flamed in sacrifice
Upon Your altar through slow-moving time.

Pain for all evil, hatred, cruelty,
For the sick of body and the sick of heart,
For all the loneliness, the lovelessness of men,

The unmeasurable loss of those that know not You –
The pain of all the world, dear God, I place
Before Your shrine.

Look down in pity and forgiveness,
Cause Your countenance to shine upon us
And give us peace.

Mollie R. Golomb

40

Yom Kippur

The tenth day of the seventh month marks the culmination of the process of repentance. A holy day on which Jews fast and remain in synagogue until the Day of Atonement ends with the setting sun and a loud triumphant blast from the Shofar.

On this day atonement shall be made for you, so as to purify you;

you shall be cleansed from all your sins before the Eternal One.

Leviticus 16.30

On this day, let us be like Moses, heavy of tongue, who had to struggle over each sound. On this day when we shall say more words than on any other day in the year, we strive to find one sentence, phrase, word, or letter that will begin here on earth and reach to the heavens.

Michael Strassfeld

Night and day, and sombrely I dress
In dark attire and consciously confess
According to the printed words, for sins

YOM KIPPUR

Suddenly remembered, all the ins
And outs, tricks, deals, and necessary lies
Regretted now, but then quite right and wise.

The benches in the *shul* are new. So this
Is what my ticket bought last year; I miss
My easy chair, this wood is hard, and I
Have changed my mind, refuse to stand and lie
About repentance. No regrets at all.
Why chain myself to a dead branch, I fall
In estimation of my neighbours who
Would have me be a liberated Jew
Ridiculing medieval ways
Keep up with them in each swift modern craze
To dedicate our souls to modern taste
To concentrate our minds on endless waste.

"Medieval" must be too new a term
For deeper, longer, truer, something firm
Within me used the word "waste". Despite years
Assimilating lack of faith, the fears
My fathers felt of God, their will to know
That vanity and greed were far below
The final aim of life will help me, too,
Atone, and be a Jew, and be a Jew.

Howard Harrison

We do not ask that our past sins may be forgiven in the sense
that their effects may be cancelled, for that is impossible; we
do not ask that our sins should not meet their punishment,
for even if the request had any meaning, we can only regard
punishment as disciplinal and advantageous. All we can and
do ask for is better insight, purer faith, fuller strength. We
want to grow in holiness of life and in the love of God. For

this we ask God's help, for this end we try by earnest prayer to realise better the true vileness of sin, how it separates us from God, and weakens and defiles us; for this end only we make repentance and seek atonement. Surely a day which is used for purposes such as these is suited for all. It involves no superstition; it is based on no assumed violation of law. As our conceptions of God, of sin, of repentance and of atonement are deepened and purified, so is the Day of Atonement deepened and purified too. Its importance and nobility rest with ourselves.

Claude G. Montefiore

I am moved by the beauty of our Yom Kippur liturgy, by the way it uses Biblical quotations to exhort us to return to God, by the way it gives expression to the poverty of humanity's attributes compared to the might and compassion of God. But the image of man as an arrogant, deceitful, hard-hearted, authoritarian, lustful, malevolent and ambitious creature does not necessarily embrace those sins and weaknesses that I find in myself, and that I imagine other women would wish to confess. For what are our over-riding sins? They are the sins which we have committed in deprecating ourselves too much, they are sins of feeling too much guilt, of failing to acknowledge the validity of our feelings; failing to act when we are treated too condescendingly or with too much contempt; for the sins which we have committed by deceiving and misleading our fellow-women, by allowing ourselves to be oppressed, by failing to be courageous, by failing to assert our authority, for being embarrassed by our age or our sex, or our jobs or our roles; and for the sins we have committed by hurting our fellow-women and men in any way.

Alexandra Wright

YOM KIPPUR

If a person says, "I will sin and repent, then I will sin again
and repent again," they are not in a position to repent.
Likewise, if they say, "I will sin, and the Day of Atonement
will atone for me", the Day of Atonement will not atone for
them.

Mishnah

If you don't catch on
that you should feel a little elevated,
you're not praying the sunset prayer.
The tune is sheer simplicity,
you're just lending a helping hand
to the sinking day.
It's a heavy responsibility.
You take a created day
and you slip it
into the archive of life,
where all our lived-out days are lying together.

The day is departing with a quiet kiss.
It lies open at your feet
while you stand saying the blessings.
You can't create anything yourself, but you
can lead the day to its end and see
clearly the smile of its going down.

See how whole it is,
not diminished for a second,
how you age with the days
that keep dawning,
how you bring your lived-out day
as a gift to eternity.

Jacob Glatstein

Glossary of Terms

Adonai	Hebrew, common synonym for the Tetra-grammaton, the holiest name of God.
Akedah	Hebrew, 'binding', used almost always to refer to the story of the Akedat Yitzchak, the Binding of Isaac, in Genesis 22.1–19.
Apocrypha	books included in the Greek and Latin translations of the Hebrew Bible but not accepted as canonical in the Hebrew Bible itself.
Baal Shem Tov	Hebrew, 'Master of the Good Name', the title given to Israel ben Eliezer, c. 1698–1760, the founder of Chasidism in the eighteenth century.
Beis Midrash	Hebrew, 'House of Study'.
Bratzlaver	referring to Rabbi Nachman of Bratzlav.
Chasidim (Hasidim)	Hebrew, 'pious ones', the followers of the Baal Shem Tov and his successors, see above.
Cheshbon ha-Nefesh	Hebrew, 'reckoning of the soul or person', e.g. personal reckoning.
Chutzpadik	Yiddish, from the Hebrew word *chutzpah*, meaning nerve, brass neck, cheek. Someone who is 'chutzpadik' would possess an abundance of chutzpah.
Clal Yisrael	Hebrew, 'all Israel', usually used to refer to the Jewish people worldwide, personified as a community.
Elul	the sixth month of the Jewish year.
Erev Rosh Hashanah	Hebrew, 'Eve of the New Year'.

184

GLOSSARY OF TERMS

Gematria	the system of assigning numerical value to the letters of the Hebrew alphabet.
Gemilut chesed	Hebrew, 'acts of loving kindness'; considered a most notable deed by the rabbis.
Hafetz Hayyim	the name given to Rabbi Yisrael Meir Kagan, 1838–1933.
Haggadah	the liturgy used by families at the ritual Seder meal on the first and second nights of Passover.
Halachah	Hebrew, 'Jewish Law', including those laws found in the Torah and in Rabbinic Literature.
Hillel	one of the great early rabbis of the first century BCE.
Hineni (hinneyni)	Hebrew, 'Here I am'.
Kavvanah	Hebrew, 'devotion', a term used to denote the correct attitude in prayer.
the Kobriner	Rabbi Moshe Kobriner, 1784–1858.
Kohelet	Hebrew name for Ecclesiastes.
Kol Nidrei	Hebrew, 'All the vows of . . .', the opening words of the first major prayer of the service on the Eve of Yom Kippur, also lending its name to the service as a whole.
L'Kiddush ha-Shem	Hebrew, 'For the sanctification of the Name', a term used to denote those who have died as martyrs.
Maggid	Hebrew, 'teller', the title given to wandering preachers in Eastern Europe renowned for their story-telling but not usually rabbis.
Marrano	Spanish, lit. 'pig'. A derogatory term used of those Spanish Jews who converted to Roman Catholicism after the decree of expulsion of 1492 so that they could remain in Spain, but who continued their Jewish observance in the strictest secrecy.
Messiah	the individual who will appear at the end of days and who is believed to be a descendant of King David.

Midrash	Hebrew, usually refers to the exegetical literature that was written by the rabbis between the first century BCE and the fourth century CE on the Hebrew Bible, and quintessentially the five books of Moses.
Minyan	Hebrew, literally 'number', but almost always the quorum of ten men traditionally required by Orthodox Jews before a service can be held.
Mishnah	Hebrew, the primary legal text of the Jewish Oral Tradition, edited by Rabbi Judah the Prince, c. 200 CE.
Mitzvot	Hebrew, 'commandments': singular 'mitzvah'.
Neilah	Hebrew, 'closing', the final service on Yom Kippur.
Neshama	Hebrew, 'soul', though it can also mean 'a person'.
Pesikta deRav Kahana	a collection of midrashim (plural of midrash) usually dated to the fifth or early sixth centuries CE.
Rambam	acronym for Rabbi Moses Maimonides.
Rashi	acronym for Rabbi Solomon ben Isaac, 1040–1105, the most popular of all the medieval Bible and Talmud commentators.
Rav	Hebrew, 'great one'; the title given to rabbis in Babylonia between the second and eighth centuries CE.
Rebbe	the Yiddish equivalent of 'rabbi'; usually used of great Hasidic rabbis as a title denoting immense respect and reverence.
Ribbono Shel Olam	Hebrew, 'Master of the Universe'.
Rosh Chodesh (hodesh)	Hebrew, literally 'Head of the Month', but usually 'new month'.
Rosh Hashanah	Hebrew, literally 'Head of the Year', but usually 'New Year'.
Sefer ha-Chinnuch	Hebrew, 'the book of education', a systematic discussion of Judaism's 613 commandments usually dated to the thirteenth century.

GLOSSARY OF TERMS

Sefirot	Hebrew, 'spheres', referring to the ten spheres containing emanations of God in Kabbalah, the Jewish mystical tradition.
Selichot	Hebrew, 'apologies', the special penitential prayers recited throughout the month of Elul, preceding the High Holy Days.
Shammai	the great contemporary and theological opponent of Hillel (see above).
Shechinah	Hebrew, 'the Divine Presence'.
Shevarim	Hebrew, one of the calls blown on the Shofar (see below) on Rosh Hashanah.
Shoah	Hebrew, literally 'whirlwind', but standard term among Jews for the Holocaust.
Shofar	Hebrew, the ram's horn blown on Rosh Hashanah and Yom Kippur.
Shul	Yiddish, commonly used word for a synagogue.
Shulchan Aruch	Hebrew, the last great systematic code of Jewish law, compiled and edited by Rabbi Joseph Karo in the sixteenth century.
Talmud	Hebrew, the great commentary on and exposition of the Mishnah (see above); there are two versions, the Jerusalem and the Babylonian, of which the latter is deemed authoritative.
Talmud Torah	Hebrew, 'the study of Torah', considered one of the highest virtues a Jew can attain.
Tanna	the name for rabbis of the Mishnaic period.
Tashlich	Hebrew, the ritual performed on the afternoon of Rosh Hashanah when sins are symbolically cast off by throwing crumbs of bread into a body of water, usually a stream or river, but occasionally also the sea.
Techine	Yiddish version of the Hebrew 'techinah', the name of a supplicatory prayer for grace, often written by a woman.
Tefillah	Hebrew, 'prayer'.
Tekiah	Hebrew, one of the blasts blown on the Shofar on Rosh Hashanah.

Tekiah gedolah	Hebrew, the loudest and longest blast blown on the Shofar on Rosh Hashanah and Yom Kippur.
Teruah	Hebrew, one of the blasts blown on the Shofar on Rosh Hashanah.
Teshuvah	Hebrew, literally 'returning', but universally used to mean 'repentance'.
Tikkun Olam	Hebrew, 'repairing the world', usually used to describe Judaism's commitment to social action, an especial hallmark of Progressive Judaism.
Tishri	the seventh month in the Hebrew calendar.
Tohu vavohu	Hebrew, the phrase used of the earth before God initiated the process of creation, usually translated as 'unformed and void'.
Torah	Hebrew, 'instruction' or 'teaching', but most commonly used as the name for the five books of Moses, and occasionally in rabbinic literature, the Hebrew Bible as a whole.
Torah lishmah	Hebrew, 'the study of Torah for its own sake', the highest motivation to study in Jewish thought.
Tzaddik	Hebrew, 'righteous one', the honorific title given to a great Hasidic rabbi, often believed by his followers to influence God by his direct appeal.
Tzedakah	Hebrew, 'righteousness', but commonly used for 'charity'.
Viddui	Hebrew, the confession that is part of the liturgy at the High Holy Day season.
Yetzer ha-Tov/ Yetzer ha-Ra	Hebrew, 'good and bad inclination'.
Yom Kippur	Hebrew, the Day of Atonement.
Zohar	Hebrew, late thirteenth century midrash, the principal work of Jewish mysticism, largely on the Torah.

Glossary of Authors and Sources

S. Y. Agnon	1888–1970. Galician-born Hebrew writer and Nobel laureate for Literature.
Arlene Agus	American feminist writer.
Yehuda Amichai	1924–2000. Israeli poet.
Sh. Ansky	1863–1920. Pen name of Shloyme Zanvl Rappoport, Russian-born scholar of Jewish folklore and author of *The Dybbuk*.
Bradley Shavit Artson	American rabbi and writer.
Baal Shem Tov	1698–1760. Title meaning Master of the Good Name, awarded to Rabbi Israel ben Eliezer, the founder of Chasidism.
Bachya ibn Pakuda	first half of the eleventh century. Spanish philosopher and ethicist.
Carol Backman	congregant, Temple Ohev Sholom, Harrisburg, PA.
Leo Baeck	1873–1956. German-born rabbi and theologian, inspirational leader of German Jewry between 1933 and 1943 when he was deported to the Terezin 'show camp'.
Hillel Bavli	1893–1961. Lithuanian-born Hebrew poet.
Chaim Nachman Bialik	1873–1934. Pioneer of modern Hebrew poetry and recognized as Israel's national poet.
Abraham Ben Yitzchak	1883–1950. Austrian-born Hebrew poet.
Eugene B. Borowitz	American rabbi, theologian and ethicist.
Ruth F. Brin	American poet, liturgist and children's writer.

E. M. Broner — (Esther M.), American feminist author and academic.

Martin Buber — 1878–1965. Austrian-born philosopher, educator and translator.

Eliezer Bugatin — Hebrew poet.

Jacob Cahan — 1881–1961. Hebrew poet and writer.

Chafetz Chaim — 1838–1933. Pseudonym of Rabbi Yisrael Meir Kagan, Polish halachist and ethicist.

Stanley F. Chyet — 1931–2002. American rabbi, writer, poet and translator.

Jonathan Cohen — American poet, translator and essayist.

Samuel S. Cohon — 1888–1959. American rabbi and academic.

Abraham Danzig — 1748–1820. Polish rabbi and halachist.

Lucy Dawidowicz — 1915–1990. American historian and scholar of the Shoah.

Samuel H. Dresner — American rabbi and theologian.

Leslie I. Edgar — 1905–1984. British Liberal rabbi.

Max Ehrmann — 1872–1945. American spiritual writer.

Albert Einstein — 1879–1955. German-born theoretical physicist and Nobel laureate for Physics.

Eleazar ben Judah of Worms — 1176–1238. Medieval talmudist and kabbalist and one of the Chasidei Ashkenaz, a group of German Jewish pietists.

Elimelech of Lizhensk — 1717–1787. Polish Hasidic rabbi and theorist.

Sue Levi Elwell — American rabbi and feminist theologian.

Alter Esselin — 1889–1974. Ukrainian-born Yiddish poet.

Emmanuel Eydoux — pen name of Roger Eisinger, French writer and historian.

Forms of Prayer — liturgy of the Reform Movement in Great Britain.

Israel Friedman of Ruzhin — 1796–1850. Russian Hasidic rabbi.

Erich Fromm — 1900–1980. German-born American psychoanalyst and social philosopher.

Abraham Geiger	1810–1874. Rabbi and theologian who was one of the founders of Reform Judaism in nineteenth-century Germany.
Levi Gersonides	1288–1344. Spanish rabbi, theologian, philosopher and commentator.
Jacob Glatstein	1896–1971. Polish-born Yiddish poet and literary critic.
Glueckel of Hameln	1646–1724. Businesswoman and diarist.
Leah Goldberg	1911–1970. Prussian-born Hebrew poet and translator.
David Goldstein	1933–1987. British rabbi, translator and oriental scholar.
Mollie R. Golomb	twentieth-century American poet.
Angela Graboys	American rabbi.
Arthur Green	American rabbi, author and educator.
Jacob L. Halevi	American rabbi and philosopher.
Judah Halevi	1075–1141. Spanish poet and philosopher.
Jules Harlow	American rabbi and liturgist.
Sidney J. Harris	1917–1986. American journalist and anthologist.
Howard Harrison	American writer.
Will Herberg	1901–1977. American intellectual and scholar.
Abraham Joshua Heschel	1907–1972. Polish-born rabbi, teacher and civil rights activist, and pre-eminent Jewish philosopher of the twentieth century.
Susannah Heschel	American academic and author.
Lawrence A. Hoffman	American rabbi, author and pre-eminent scholar of Reform liturgy.
John Hollander	American poet and literary critic.
Vicki Hollander	American rabbi and poet.
Arthur C. Jacobs	1937–1994. Scottish poet and translator.
Louis Jacobs	1920–2006. British rabbi, eminent scholar and theologian.
Morris Joseph	1848–1930. British Reform rabbi and theologian.

Eleazar Kallir	late seventh century Palestinian Hebrew poet.
Mordecai M. Kaplan	1881–1983. American rabbi, theologian and founder of Reconstructionist Judaism.
Aleph Katz	1898–1969. Pen name of Morris Abraham Katz. Polish-born Yiddish poet.
Grenville Kleiser	1868–1953. American writer and anthologist.
Abraham Isaac Kook	1865–1935. Latvian-born theologian, mystic and Bible scholar; the first Ashkenazi chief rabbi of mandatory Palestine.
Lawrence Kushner	American rabbi and mystic.
Joseph Leftwich	1892–1984. British poet, biographer and literary critic.
Denise Levertov	1923–1997. English-born poet and political activist.
Primo Levi	1919–1987. Italian Shoah survivor, chemist and author.
Levi Yitzchak of Berditchev	1740–1810. Hasidic rabbi and leader.
Liberal Jewish Prayer Book	the first prayer book of English Liberal Judaism, edited by Rabbi Dr Israel I. Mattuck.
Deborah E. Lipstadt	American historian of the Shoah.
Raphael Loewe	British academic, author and poet.
Isaac Luria	1534–1572. Spanish-born mystic and poet.
Machzor	prayer book for the High Holy Days and the Pilgrimage Festivals.
Machzor Ruach Chadashah	the current High Holy Day prayer book of English Liberal Judaism.
Maharil	1365–1427. Acronym for rabbi Jacob ben Moses Moelin. German talmudist and authority on Jewish law.
Moses Maimonides	1135–1204. Spanish rabbi, physician and philosopher.
Israel I. Mattuck	1883–1954. First rabbi of English Liberal Judaism.

Yitzchak Meir of Ger   1798–1866. Hasidic rabbi and talmudist.

Marshall T. Meyer   1930–1993. American rabbi and human rights activist.

Midrash   the corpus of rabbinic homiletical Bible interpretation.

Zelda Mishkofsky   1914–1984. Ukrainian-born Hebrew poet.

Mishnah   the primary text of Jewish Oral law.

Kadya Molodowsky   1894–1975. Russian Yiddish poet.

Lily H. Montagu   1873–1963. Social activist and co-founder of English Liberal Judaism.

Claude G. Montefiore   1858–1938. Scholar, philanthropist and co-founder of English Liberal Judaism.

Moses ben Abraham of Premsla   c. 1551–c. 1606. Rabbi and scholar.

Moses ibn Ezra   c. 1055/1060–c. 1138. Spanish philosopher, poet and linguist.

Nachman of Bratzlav   1772–1810. Ukrainian Hasidic rabbi and grandson of the Baal Shem Tov.

Howard Nemerov   1920–1991. American poet.

Jacob Neusner   American rabbi and scholar.

Louis I. Newman   1893–1972. British rabbi and scholar.

Mary Oliver   American poet.

Toybe Pan   seventeenth century Yiddish poet, wife of Jacob Pan.

David Patterson   1922–2005. Scholar of Jewish and Hebrew literature, translator and author.

I. L. Peretz   1852–1915. Yiddish author and playright.

Debbie Perlman   1951–2002. American psalmist.

Marge Piercy   American poet.

Marjorie Pizer   Australian poet.

Rachel   1890–1931. Pen name of Rachel Bluwstein Sela, Hebrew poet.

Laura Rappaport   American writer.

John D. Rayner   1924–2005. Pre-eminent British Liberal rabbi, scholar, theologian and liturgist.

Abraham Reisen	Russian-born Yiddish poet.
Charles Reznikoff	1894–1976. American poet.
Jack Riemer	American rabbi, liturgist and anthologist.
David Rokeach	1916–1985. Hebrew poet.
Israel Salanter	1810–1883. Lithuanian rabbi, founder of the Musar movement in Orthodox Judaism.
Elizabeth Tikvah Sarah	British rabbi.
Arnold Schoenberg	1874–1951. Austrian-born composer.
Harold M. Schulweis	American rabbi and author.
Frances Weinman Schwartz	American author.
Howard Schwartz	American folklorist, story-teller and author.
Steven S. Schwarzschild	1924–1989. American rabbi, theologian and philosopher.
Seder Rav Amram	the earliest collection of Jewish liturgy, dated to the ninth century CE and bearing the name of Amram Gaon, d. 875, head of the Sura academy in Babylon.
Sefer ha-Chinnuch	thirteenth-century text discussing the 613 commandments of Jewish law.
Hannah Senesh	1921–1944. Hungarian-born Israeli, murdered by the Nazis following a failed mission to save the Jews of Hungary.
Sephardi Machzor	High Holy Day prayer book of the Spanish and Portuguese Jews' Congregation, London.
Shin Shalom	1904–1990. Pen name of Shalom Joseph Shapira. Polish-born Hebrew poet.
Alice Shalvi	German-born Israeli academic and religious feminist.
Rami Shapiro	American rabbi and author.
Shulchan Aruch	codification of Jewish law authored by Rabbi Joseph Karo in the sixteenth century.
Siddur Lev Chadash	the current daily, Sabbath and Festival prayer book of English Liberal Judaism.

GLOSSARY OF AUTHORS AND SOURCES

Siddur Rabbi Yaabetz	eighteenth-century prayer book edited by Rabbi Jacob ben Zvi Emden.
Danny Siegel	American rabbi and poet.
Vivian Simmons	1886–1970. British rabbi.
Isaac Bashevis Singer	1904–1991. Polish-born Yiddish writer and novelist and Nobel laureate for Literature.
Solomon ibn Gabirol	c. 1021–1058. Pre-eminent Hebrew poet and philosopher of the Golden Age of Spain.
Joseph B. Soloveitchik	1903–1993. Russian-born rabbi, talmudist and philosopher.
Chaim Stern	1930–2001. American rabbi and liturgist.
Michael Strassfeld	American rabbi and author.
Talmud	the commentary to the Mishnah, found in two versions, the Jerusalem and the Babylonian, redacted between the third and sixth centuries CE.
Malka Heifetz Tussman	1896–1987. Ukrainian-born poet.
David Vogel	1891–1944. Russian-born poet.
Albert Vorspan	leading American Reform lay leader and social activist.
Elie Wiesel	Shoah survivor, author and Nobel peace laureate.
Leon Wieseltier	American writer, critic and magazine editor.
Alexandra Wright	British rabbi.
Yehoash	1870–1927. Pen name of Solomon Blumgarten, Lithuanian-born Yiddish poet.
Natan Zach	Hebrew poet.
Israel Zangwill	1864–1926. British writer and humorist.
Aaron Zeitlin	1898–1973. Belarus-born scholar of Hebrew literature and poet.
S.Y. Zevin	Chasidic rabbi and author.
Israel Zoberman	American rabbi.

Acknowledgements

Every effort has been made to secure copyright permission from the authors cited or their publisher. We will be happy to rectify any errors of omission in subsequent printings.

1 New Moon of Elul

"Prayer for the New Month" by Rabbi Vicki Hollander. © Vicki Hollander. Used by permission of the author.

"We the collected bless . . ." by E. M. Broner. *Bringing Home the Light: A Jewish Woman's Handbook of Rituals*. San Francisco, Tulsa: Council Oak Books, 1999.

"Traditionally we say . . ." quoting Rabbi Jack Riemer. Used by permission of the author.

2 Renewal

"Teach me, my God . . ." by Leah Goldberg, translated by Rabbi John D. Rayner. Reprinted by permission of Liberal Judaism.

"Rabbi Bunam taught . . ." by Martin Buber. This and all subsequent Buber texts are taken from *Tales of the Hasidim, The Early Masters, The Later Masters*. New York: Schocken Books Inc., 1947, 1948.

"Ruler of the universe! . . ." by Debbie Perlman. *Flames to Heaven: New Psalms for Healing and Praise*. Wilmette, IL: Rad Publishers, 1998.

ACKNOWLEDGEMENTS

"Said the Bratzlaver ..." by Louis I. Newman. *Maggidim and Hasidim: Their Wisdom. A New Anthology of the Parables, Folk-Tales, Fables, Aphorisms, Epigrams, Sayings, Anecdotes, Proverbs, and Exegetical Interpretations of the Leading Maggidim (Folk-Preachers) and the Hasidic Masters and Their Disciples.* New York: Schocken Books Inc., 1972.

"The Last Word" by Rabbi Harold M. Schulweis. From *Finding Each Other in Judaism*. © 2001 by UAHC Press. Reprinted with permission of URJ Press.

3 Hope

"O give thanks . . ." by Rabbi Chaim Stern in *Gates of Prayer: The New Union Prayerbook* © 1975 by Central Conference of American Rabbis. Used by permission of Central Conference of American Rabbis. All rights reserved.

"When evil darkens our world ..." by Rabbi John D. Rayner. Reprinted by permission of Liberal Judaism.

"Lord we thank You ..." from *Forms of Prayer*. Reprinted with permission of The Movement for Reform Judaism.

"O God, give me strength . . ." by Eliezer Bugatin, translated by Rabbi Chaim Stern, from *Ha-avodah she balev*. Used by permission of the Israel Movement for Progressive Judaism.

"Only the hopeful ..." by David Rokeach, translated by Rabbi Chaim Stern. Reprinted by permission of Liberal Judaism.

"Hope" by Carol Backman. From *Covenant of the Heart – Prayers, Poems and Meditations from the Women of Reform Judaism*. National Federation of Temple Sisterhoods, USA, 1993.

4 Belief

"There is a paradox . . ." by Rabbi John D. Rayner. Reprinted by permission of Liberal Judaism.

"Faith is the life-breath of religion" by Samuel S. Cohon. From *Essays in Jewish Theology* (1987). Reprinted with permission of The Hebrew Union College Press, Cincinnati.

ACKNOWLEDGEMENTS

"For me, encountering God . . ." by Arlene Agus. *Two Jews, Three Opinions: A Collection of 20th century American Jewish quotations*, ed. Sandee Brawarsky and Deborah Mark. New York: Perigee, 1998.

8 Doubt

"I have no idea to whom . . ." by Kadya Molodowsky. Translation © Rabbi Dr Charles H. Middleburgh.

"The Sassover Rebbe" translated by Chaim Stern in *Day by Day*, ed. Chaim Stern © 1998 Central Conference of American Rabbis. Used by permission of Central Conference of American Rabbis. All rights reserved.

"A disciple asked the Baal Shem . . ." by Martin Buber. As previously.

"Resistance to the word . . ." by Will Herberg. From *Judaism and Modern Man*, reprinted by permission of Karen Jones.

"I find it is Yom Kippur, . . ." by Arthur C. Jacobs. Reprinted by permission of The Movement for Reform Judaism.

"The difficulty for us . . ." by Vivian Simmons. From *The Path of Life*. Reprinted by permission from Vallentine, Mitchell Publishers, London.

9 Nature

"In the beginning . . ." by Ruth F. Brin from *Harvest: Collected Poems and Prayers*. © 1986, 1999 by Ruth Firestone Brin. Reprinted by permission of Holy Cow! Press, www.holycowpress.org.

"Master of the Universe . . ." a prayer taught by Rabbi Nachman to his scribe, Rabbi Nathan Sternhartz.

"Who made the world . . .", by Mary Oliver. *New and Selected Poems*. Boston, MA: Beacon Press, 1992.

"Summer's Elegy" by Howard Nemerov. Reprinted by permission of Margaret Nemerov.

"Beauty" by Alter Esselin. *The Golden Peacock: A Worldwide*

Treasury of Yiddish Poetry, compiled, translated and edited by Joseph Leftwich. New York: Thomas Yoseloff, 1961.

"Rabbi Nachman of Bratzlav" by Aleph Katz. *The Golden Peacock: A Worldwide Treasury of Yiddish Poetry*, compiled, translated and edited by Joseph Leftwich. New York: Thomas Yoseloff, 1961.

10 God

"When men were children . . ." Ruth F. Brin, excerpts from *Harvest: Collected Poems and Prayers.* © 1986, 1999 by Ruth Firestone Brin. Reprinted by permission of Holy Cow! Press, www.holycowpress. org.

"Our ancestors acclaimed . . ." by Rabbi Mordecai M. Kaplan. *Kol Haneshamah: Mahzor Leyamim Nora'im.* The Reconstructionist Press, 101 Greenwood Ave, Ste 430, Jenkintown, PA USA 19046. fax: 1-215-885-5603, phone: 1-877-JRF.PUBS, email: press@jrf.org, website: www.jrfbookstore.org.

"Praise Me, says God . . ." by Aaron Zeitlin, translated by E. Goldsmith.

"O, Thou my God . . ." by Arnold Schoenberg, translated by Dika Newlin. Reprinted by permission from *The Reconstructionist*, Volume 24, Number 19.

11 Prayer

"How do I learn to pray . . ." by Rabbi Steven S. Schwarzschild. Reprinted by permission of The Movement for Reform Judaism.

"Normally, we are compelled . . ." by Rabbi Leslie I. Edgar. Reprinted by permission of Liberal Judaism.

"I have always found prayer . . ." By Rabbi Israel I. Mattuck. Reprinted by permission of Liberal Judaism.

"Our father, our King . . ." by Rabbi David Goldstein. Reprinted by permission of Berry Goldstein.

ACKNOWLEDGEMENTS

12 Reconciliation

"The Tzanzer Rebbe . . ." by Martin Buber. As previously.

"The Rabbi of Lelov . . ." by Martin Buber. As previously.

13 The Journey

"If you have no past . . ." by I. L. Peretz. *Kol Haneshamah: Mahzor Leyamim Nora'im*. The Reconstructionist Press, 101 Greenwood Ave, Ste 430, Jenkintown, PA USA 19046. fax: 1-215-885-5603, phone: 1-877-JRF.PUBS, email: press@jrf.org, website: www.jrfbookstore. org

"A Prayer" © by Max Erhmann. Used by permission of Bell & Son Publishing, LLC. All rights reserved.

"Let me not swerve . . ." by Hillel Bavli, translated by Rabbi Norman Tarnor. © The Rabbinical Assembly, used by permission of the publisher.

"Psalm" by Abraham Ben-Yitzchak, translated by Arthur C. Jacobs.

"So many people . . ." by Rabbi Dr Leo Baeck, cited in Machzor Ruach Chadashah, p. 162.

"Is it really the end? . . ." by Rachel, translated by Rabbi Sidney Greenberg.

14 The Years Pass By

"A man doesn't have time . . ." from *The Selected Poetry of Yehuda Amichai*, translated by Stephen Mitchell and Chana Bloch. © 1996 by Stephen Mitchell and Chana Bloch. Published by the University of California Press, Berkeley and Los Angeles.

"A Commentary on Kohelet" by Rabbi Chaim Stern, from an unpublished text.

"We learn, slowly . . ." by Sidney J. Harris. From *Living Thoughts: Inspiration, insight, and wisdom from sources throughout the ages*, edited by Bernard S. Raskas. Bridgport, CT: Hartmore House, 1976.

"A Prayer of the Rabbis" by Rabbi Lawrence Kushner. Based on the Talmud. Used by permission of the author.

15 Full Moon of Elul

"Without telling his teacher . . ." by Martin Buber. As previously

"It is appropriate to study . . ." adapted by the Editors from a text by S. Y. Agnon.

"A Prayer for A. A. Wolmark" by Joseph Leftwich. *Along the Years*. London: Robert Anscombe and Co., 1937.

16 Study

"Talk of rewards . . ." by Frances Weinman Schwartz and Rabbi Eugene B. Borowitz. © Frances Weinman Schwartz and Eugene Borowitz, published by The Jewish Publication Society and reprinted with the permission of the publisher.

"*Talmud Torah* . . ." by Rabbi John D. Rayner. Reprinted by permission of Liberal Judaism.

"You can learn something . . ." by Martin Buber. As previously.

"The Hafetz Hayyim said . . ." by Louis I. Newman. As previously.

17 Tikkun Olam

"Each lifetime is the pieces . . ." by Rabbi Lawrence Kushner. Used by permission of the author.

"To open eyes . . ." by Emmanuel Eydoux, translated by Rabbi Professor Jonathan Magonet, and reprinted with his permission.

"I believe that God is the source . . ." by Rabbi Marshall T. Meyer. © Congregation B'nai Jeshurun. Used by permission of Naomi Meyer.

"The Jewish passion . . ." by Albert Vorspan. From *Start Worrying: Details to Follow*. © 1991 by URJ Press. Reprinted with permission of URJ Press.

"A Techine for Yom Kippur" by Alice Shalvi. Used by permission of Professor Alice Shalvi.

ACKNOWLEDGEMENTS

18 Personal Responsibility

"Once on Rosh Hashanah . . ." by Martin Buber. *The Hidden Light.* Frankfurt: Rütten and Loening, 1924.

"There are many fine things . . ." by Grenville Kleiser. © 1994 by Central Conference of American Rabbis. Used by permission of Central Conference of American Rabbis. All rights reserved.

"God give us the strength . . ." by Angela Graboys and Laura Rappaport, from "ROW Service", an unpublished manuscript, Hebrew Union College – Jewish Institute of Religion.

"Rabbi Bunam said to his Hasidim . . ." by Martin Buber. *Tales of the Hasidim* as previously.

"Peace" by Rabbi Rami Shapiro. © Rami Shapiro. Used by permission of the author.

19 Self-Examination

"Today we stand before the Mirror . . ." by Rabbi Rami Shapiro. © Rami Shapiro. Used by permission of the author.

"The Rabbi of Berditchev . . ." by Martin Buber. As previously.

"Man is the only creature . . ." by Erich Fromm. *Man for Himself: An inquiry into the psychology of ethics.* Oxford: Routledge Classics, 2008.

20 Good and Bad Inclination

"A villager lamented . . ." by Louis I. Newman. *Hasidic Anthology: Tales of the Hasidim.* New York: Schocken Books Inc., 1963.

"When we do something . . ." by Rabbi Israel I. Mattuck. Reprinted by permission of Liberal Judaism.

"With the Rabbis we may speak . . ." by Rabbi John D. Rayner. Reprinted by permission of Liberal Judaism.

21 Humility

"To begin with oneself . . ." attributed to Martin Buber.

"Hineni" by Stanley F. Chyet in *CCAR Journal: The Reform Jewish Quarterly*, Volume LI, No. 2 Issue: Two Hundred © 2004 Central Conference of American Rabbis. Used by permission of Central Conference of American Rabbis. All rights reserved.

"Te Deum" by Charles Reznikoff. From *The Poems of Charles Reznikoff: 1918–1975*, edited by Seamus Cooney. Reprinted by permission of Black Sparrow Books, an imprint of David R. Godine, Publisher, Inc. Copyright © 2005 by Charles Reznikoff, edited by Seamus Cooney.

"God on high . . ." a Marrano prayer from Language of Faith: A Selection from the Most Expressive Jewish Prayers, gathered and edited by Nahum. N. Glatzer. New York: Schocken Books Inc., 1975.

22 Human Nature

"Is there a person anywhere . . ." by Rabbi Abraham Danzig, adapted by Rabbi Jules Harlow. Copyright © The Rabbinical Assembly, used by permission of the publisher.

"Guard me, Oh God . . ." by Shin Shalom, translated by Ruth Finer Mintz.

"Each of us has a name . . ." by Zelda Mishkofsky, translated by Rabbi Chaim Stern. Reprinted by permission of Liberal Judaism.

"Alone among God's creatures . . ." by Rabbi John D. Rayner. Reprinted by permission of Liberal Judaism.

23 Selichot

"The happenings of this world . . ." attributed to Martin Buber.

"In darkening shade . . ." by Ruth F. Brin. Excerpts from *Harvest: Collected Poems and Prayers*. © 1986, 1999 by Ruth Firestone Brin. Reprinted by permission of Holy Cow! Press, www.holycowpress.org.

ACKNOWLEDGEMENTS

"You know the thoughts of men . . ." by Bachya ibn Pakuda, translated by Rabbi Dr Charles H. Middleburgh.

24 The Will to Change

"Each evening before he went to sleep . . ." by Samuel H. Dresner. From *Levi Yitzchak of Berditchev, Portrait of a Chasidic Master*. Bridgport, CT: Hartmore House, 1974.

"Of the Chasidic Saint . . ." attributed to Martin Buber.

25 Wisdom

"My father used to say . . ." by Professor Susannah Heschel, from *The Invisible Thread: A portrait of Jewish American Women*, edited by Diana Bletter and Lori Grinker. Philadelphia: JPSA, 1989.

26 Human Suffering

"Ten trials were inflicted . . ." by Rabbi Rami Shapiro. © Rami Shapiro. Used by permission of the author.

"A god once commanded us . . ." by Leah Goldberg. Translation by Robert Friend © Jean Shapiro Cantu; reprinted by permission.

"If we could hang . . ." by Martin Buber. From *Ten Rungs*. New York: Schocken Books Inc., 1947.

"In times of darkness . . ." by Jacob L. Halevi in *CCAR Journal: The Reform Jewish Quarterly*, Volume LI, No. 2 Issue: Two Hundred © 2004 Central Conference of American Rabbis. Used by permission of Central Conference of American Rabbis. All rights reserved.

"The Penitential Season . . ." by Abrahan Reisen. *The Golden Peacock: A Worldwide Treasury of Yiddish Poetry*, compiled, translated and edited by Joseph Leftwich. London: Robert Anscombe and Co., 1939.

27 Remembering the Dead

"It is customary . . ." by the Editors, based on S. Y. Agnon.

"Immortality . . ." by Harold M. Schulweis. From *What Happens after I Die?*, edited by Rifat Sonsino and Daniel B. Syme. © 1990 by UAHC Press. Reprinted with permission of URJ Press.

"I had thought that your death . . ." by Marjorie Pizer. Used by permission of the author.

"The difference between the living . . ." by Leon Wieseltier. *Kaddish*. New York: Alfred A. Knopf, Inc., 1998.

"Strange is our situation . . ." adapted by Rabbi Chaim Stern from an original passage by Albert Einstein.

"There are stars . . ." by Hannah Senesh, from her Diary.

28 Mystery

"I do not know your ways . . ." by Malka Heifetz Tussman, translated by the Editors.

"Behind every certainty . . ." by Rabbi Dr Leo Baeck. *This People Israel*, translated by Rabbi Dr Albert H. Friedlander. London: W. H. Allen, 1965.

"Indeed, it is from within . . ." by Rabbi Arthur Green. 1994 Samuel H. Goldensohn Lecture, Hebrew Union College, Cincinatti.

"Gathering the Sparks" by Howard Schwartz, reprinted from *Gathering the Sparks: Poems 1965–1979*, © 1979 by Howard Schwartz. All rights reserved. Used by permission of the author.

"To pray is to regain . . ." by Abraham Joshua Heschel. From *I Asked for Wonder: A Spiritual Anthology*, edited by Abraham Joshua Heschel and Samuel H. Dresner. New York: The Crossroad Publishing Company, 1983.

"Out of the depths . . ." by Jacob Cahan, translated by Rabbi Chaim Stern.

"The Thread" by Denise Levertov, from *POEMS* 1960–67, © 1966 by Denise Levertov. Reprinted by permission of New Directions Publishing Corp.

ACKNOWLEDGEMENTS

29 Autumn is Coming

"Summer is dying . . ." by Chaim Nachman Bialik, translated by the Editors.

"On Autumn Nights" © Copyright in the original Hebrew, the estate of David Vogel. English Translation Copyright © Institute for the Translation of Hebrew Literature.

"Existence will remain . . ." adapted by the Editors from a passage by Martin Buber.

"Softly, Like a murmuring . . ." by Joseph Leftwich. *Along the Years.* London: Robert Anscombe and Co., 1937.

"I saw a white bird . . ." by Natan Zach, translated by Robert Mezey.

"The quality of life . . ." by Rabbi John D. Rayner. Reprinted by permission of Liberal Judaism.

"Now is the time for turning . . ." by Rabbi Jack Riemer. Used by permission of the author.

30 Creation

"The stars of heaven . . ." by Rabbi Chaim Stern in *On the Doorposts of your House*, © 1994 Central Conference of American Rabbis. Used by permission of Central Conference of American Rabbis. All rights reserved.

"The essence of the Jewish conception . . ." adapted from an original passage by Albert Einstein.

"After the Great Maggid's death . . ." by Martin Buber. *Tales of the Hasidim: Early Masters*, as previously.

"The Sun" by Mary Oliver. *New and Selected Poems*, as previously.

"In the Beginning" by Primo Levi. From *Collected Poems*, translated by Ruth Feldman and Brian Swan. London: Faber and Faber, 1988.

"My thoughts awaken me to see You . . ." by Moses ibn Ezra, translated by Professor Raymond P. Scheindlin, adapted by the Editors. From *The Gazelle: Medieval Poems on God, Israel and the Soul*. Oxford University Press, 1999.

31 Erev Rosh Hashanah

"As we Jews now enter . . ." by Elie Wiesel. © 1997 Elie Wiesel. Reprinted by permission of the author.

"Rosh Ha-Shanah" by Rabbi Elizabeth Tikvah Sarah. Reprinted by permission of Liberal Judaism.

"A woman and a Jew . . ." by Marge Piercy. From *The Art of Blessing the Day*. New York: Alfred A. Knopf Inc., 1989.

"The eve of Rosh Hashanah . . ." from *The Selected Poetry of Yehuda Amichai*, translated by Stephen Mitchell and Chana Bloch. © 1996 by Stephen Mitchell and Chana Bloch. Published by the University of California Press.

"At the New Year" by John Hollander. From *Selected Poetry*. New York: Alfred A. Knopf Inc., 1993.

32 Rosh Hashanah

"The God of judgement . . ." by Rabbi Arthur Green. © 2000 Rabbi Arthur Green. Woodstock, VT: Jewish Lights Publishing. Permission granted by Jewish Lights Publishing, www.jewishlights.com.

"Remember us for life!" by Jules Harlow. © The Rabbinical Assembly, used by permission of the publisher.

"This is the autumn . . ." by Charles Reznikoff. From *The Poems of Charles Reznikoff: 1918–1975*, edited by Seamus Cooney. Reprinted by permission of Black Sparrow Books, an imprint of David R. Godine, Publisher, Inc. Copyright © 2005 by Charles Reznikoff, edited by Seamus Cooney.

"Footnote to a Rosh Hashanah Prayer" by Ruth F. Brin. Excerpts from *Harvest: Collected Poems and Prayers*. © 1986, 1999 by Ruth Firestone Brin. Reprinted by permission of Holy Cow! Press, www. holycowpress.org.

"One year . . ." by Rabbi S. Y. Zevin. Reproduced with permission of the copyright holders, ArtScroll/Mesorah Publications Ltd.

ACKNOWLEDGEMENTS

33 The Shofar

"The ram's horn cut off . . ." by Israel Zoberman in *CCAR Journal: The Reform Jewish Quarterly*, vol. LI, *Poetry from the Fifty Years of the CCAR Journal*. Used by permission of Central Conference of American Rabbis. All rights reserved.

"Once, when Rabbi Bunam . . ." by Martin Buber. As previously.

"The mystics have their own . . ." by Louis Jacobs. Taken from *A Guide to Rosh Hashanah*, 1969. Extract courtesy of the *Jewish Chronicle*.

"Rabbi Pinchas Shapiro . . ." by David Patterson. Reprinted from *The Greatest Jewish Stories Ever Told*, copyright © 1997, 2001 by David Patterson. By arrangement with Jonathan David Publishers, Inc., Middle Village New York 11379. www.jdbooks.com.

"The fat time of the year . . ." by Howard Nemerov. Reprinted by permission of Margaret Nemerov.

"The Shofar Calls" by Ruth F. Brin. Excerpts from *Harvest: Collected Poems and Prayers*. © 1986, 1999 by Ruth Firestone Brin. Reprinted by permission of Holy Cow! Press, www.holycowpress.org.

"From year to year the need becomes . . ." by Rabbi John D. Rayner. Reprinted by permission of Liberal Judaism.

34 Tashlich

"God, I know that the wrongs . . ." by Jonathan Cohen. *Renew Our Days, A Prayer-Cycle for Days of Awe*, edited and translated by Rabbi Ronald Aigen. Hampstead, Quebec: Congregation Dorshei Emet, 2001.

"It was Rosh Hashanah . . ." from *Tashlich*, an unpublished text, translated from the Yiddish by Isaac Bashevis Singer and Cecil Hemley.

"This afternoon my family . . ." by Rabbi Sue Levi Elwell. Used by permission of the author.

35 Community

"We Jews are a community . . ." attributed to Martin Buber.

"If you think you can live . . ." by Rabbi Chaim Stern in *Day by Day – Reflections on the Themes of the Torah*, © 1998 Central Conference of American Rabbis. Used by permission of Central Conference of American Rabbis. All rights reserved.

"A Talmudic adage . . ." from *The Journey Home* by Lawrence A. Hoffman. © 2002 by Lawrence A. Hoffman. Reprinted by permission of Beacon Press, Boston.

"Once, the Baal Shem . . ." by Martin Buber. As previously.

36 Tzedakah

"One can always find warm hearts . . ." by Leo Baeck. *Forms of Prayer for the Days of Awe*. London: The Movement for Reform Judaism, 1994.

"Rabbi Yehuda used to say . . ." by Rabbi Danny Siegel. Used by permission of the author.

37 Sin

"A Vocabulary of Sin" adapted by Rabbi Dr Andrew Goldstein from a piece by Rabbi Dr Louis Jacobs.

"My God, I know . . ." by Solomon ibn Gabirol. From *Selected Poems of Solomon ibn Gabirol*, translated by Peter Cole. Princeton University Press, 2001.

"*Ribbono shel olam* . . ." by Rabbi Abraham Danzig, translated by Rabbi Jack Riemer and used with his permission.

38 Repentance

"Not only do we fail . . ." by Deborah E. Lipstadt. From *The Jewish Spectator*, Fall 1993.

"An ignorant villager . . ." by Louis I. Newman. *Maggidim and Hasidim*, as previously.

ACKNOWLEDGEMENTS

"What is the meaning of the word . . ." by Rabbi Joseph B. Soloveitchik. From *On Repentance in the Thought and Oral Discourses of Rabbi Joseph B. Soloveitchik*, edited by Pinchas Peli. Jerusalem: Oroth Publishing House, 1980.

"Father, King" by Toybe Pan. Reprinted from *Seder Tkhines: The Forgotten Book of Common Prayer for Jewish Women*, © 2004, edited and translated by Devra Kay, published by The Jewish Publication Society and reprinted with the permission of the publisher.

"The power of repentance . . ." by Rabbi Professor Jacob Neusner. From *Rabbinic Judaism*. Montreal: McGill-Queen's University Press, 2002.

39 Kol Nidrei

"Yom Kippur Eve" by Zelda Mishkofsky. From *The Spectacular Difference*, translated by Marcia Falk. New York: HUC Press, 2004.

"Sin and Repentance" by Rabbi Mordecai M. Kaplan. *Kol Haneshamah: Mahzor Leyamim Nora'im*. The Reconstructionist Press, 101 Greenwood Ave, Ste 430, Jenkintown, PA USA 19046. fax: 1-215-885-5603, phone: 1-877-JRF.PUBS, email: press@jrf.org, website: www.jrfbookstore.org.

"Once, just before New Year's, . . ." by Martin Buber. As previously.

"Erev Yom Kippur" by Mollie R. Golomb. Reprinted from *The Yom Kippur Anthology*, © 1971 Philip Goodman, editor, published by The Jewish Publication Society and reprinted with the permission of the publisher.

40 Yom Kippur

"On this day, let we be like Moses" by Rabbi Michael Strassfeld. © Michael Strassfeld. Reprinted by permission.

"Night and day . . ." by Howard Harrison. Reprinted from *The Yom Kippur Anthology*, © 1971 Philip Goodman, editor, published by The Jewish Publication Society and reprinted with the permission of the publisher

"I am moved by the beauty . . ." by Rabbi Alexandra Wright. Used with the permission of the author.

"If you don't catch on . . ." by Jacob Glatstein, translated by Ruth Whitman. *Kol Haneshamah: Mahzor Leyamim Nora'im.* The Reconstructionist Press, 101 Greenwood Ave, Ste 430, Jenkintown, PA USA 19046. fax: 1-215-885-5603, phone: 1-877-JRF.PUBS, email: press@jrf.org, website: www.jrfbookstore.org.